Someone Saved My Life Today

Someone Saved My Life Today

Collected Papers on Psychoanalysis, Literature and Philosophy of Paul Schimmel

Paul Schimmel

International Psychoanalytic Books (IPBooks)
New York • http://www.IPBooks.net

Someone Save My Life Today

Published by IPBooks, Queens, NY
Online at: www.IPBooks.net

Copyright © 2022 Paul Schimmel

All rights reserved. This book may not be reproduced, transmitted, or stored, in whole or in part by any means, including graphic, electronic, or mechanical without the express permission of the author and/or publisher, except in the case of brief quotations embodied in critical articles and reviews.

Cover image of Sphinx and pyramids used under license from Shutterstock.com

ISBN: 978-1-956864-20-5

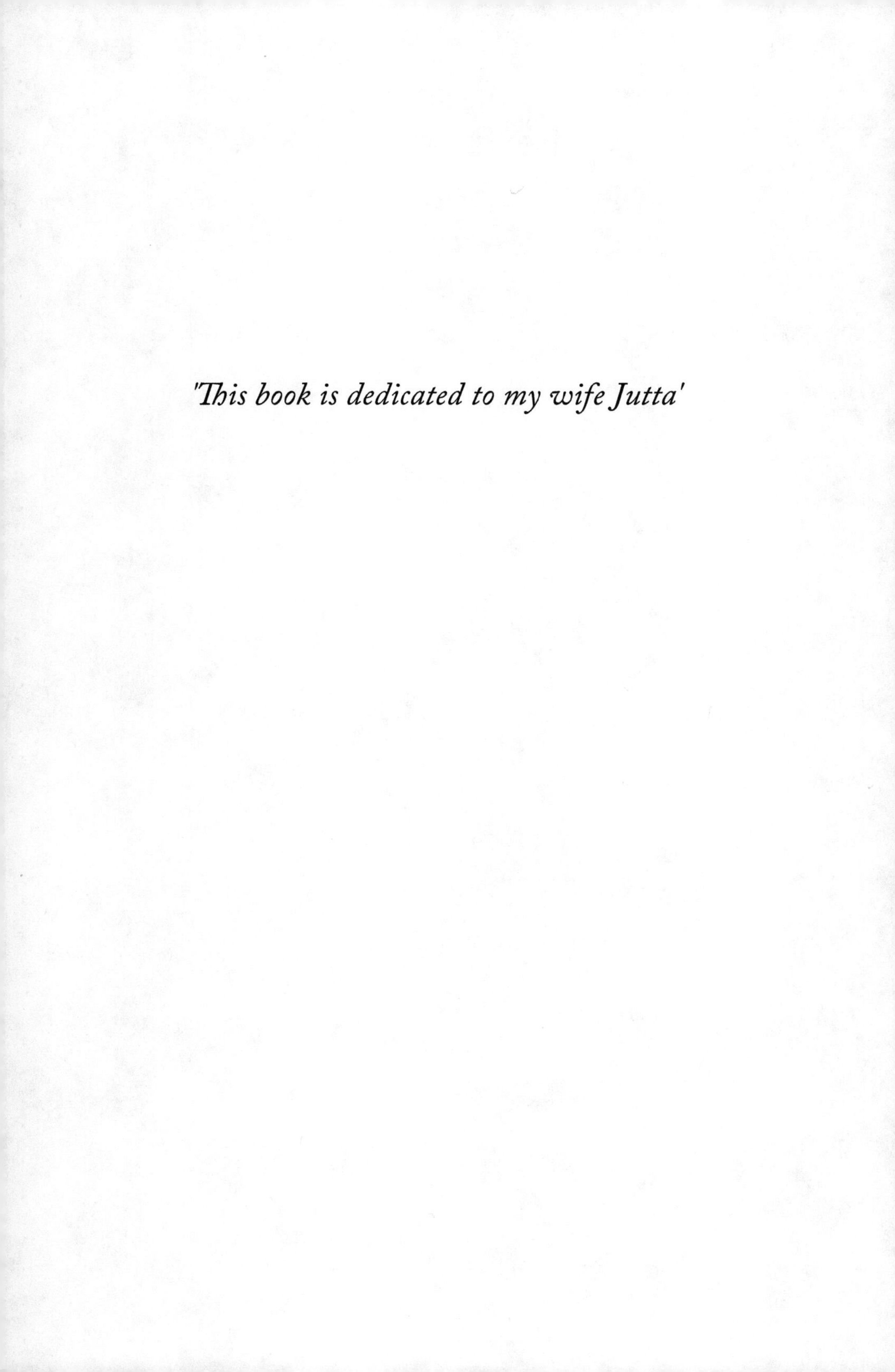

'This book is dedicated to my wife Jutta'

Contents

May 6th, 1895

a poem for Freud's 39th birthday

> 'Like a long-legged fly upon the stream
> His mind moves upon silence'
>
> —W.B. Yeats

Vienna, 19 Berggasse. Freud, wired
at work on his *Project*, pacing into
the night. A house of complete silence;
only, his own nerves' electric hum.
Now, past midnight, the 6th of May,
he lights, after months of abstinence,
a cigar. It is his birthday. Smoke curls
around antiquities; the riddle of his sphinx.
His thoughts fly, not to the children
dreaming in silent rooms, or the space
warm beside Martha deeply asleep;
they fly first to another city, leaping
borders, Pegasus at light speed;
they are *quanta* traveling above
houses, hilltops, farmyards, fields,
a land warming from winter; across
the centre of Europe, crashing
the *contact barriers* to Wilhelm,
friend, alter ego, other self;
who else can help him now?

Introduction

The late Neville Symington of the Australian and British Psychoanalytic Societies placed great importance upon freedom and the freedom to speak. He did so without fear or favour, and not always to the appreciation of others. It has taken me many years to learn this lesson of freedom.

A brief tribute to Neville is included at the end of this book. As I write there, I mined Neville's work for everything I could get.

The book begins with a poem for Freud's birthday: *May 6, 1895*, previously published in my book, *Sigmund Freud's discovery of psychoanalysis: conquistador and thinker.*

Next is a recent and unpublished essay 'An elegy for mourning and "subjecticide".' The word 'subjecticide' is taken from Christopher Bollas's brilliant paper of 2015, 'Psychoanalysis in the age of bewilderment: On the return of the oppressed'.

This collection begins with two early papers, 'Medicine and the manic defence', published in *The Australia and New Zealand Journal of Psychiatry*, and 'Psychoanalysis: what is it and why is it hated'.

Two papers published in *The British Journal of Psychotherapy*, on W.B. Yeats, 'It is myself that I remake': W.B. Yeats's self-construction in life and poetry, and T.S. Eliot, 'In my end is my beginning': T.S. Eliot's *The Waste Land* and after', follow.

Interposed between these two is 'Psychoanalysis and psychotherapy: a personal view'. There were few things that I disagreed with Neville Symington about, but one was his sharp delineation between psychoanalysis and psychotherapy which, I believe, doesn't do justice to the complexity of the situation. My reasoning is argued in 'Psychoanalysis and psychotherapy: a personal view', written as part of a debate in *Psychoanalysis Downunder*, the online journal of the Australian Psychoanalytic Society. Another issue was Neville's view that psychoanalysis is not a science. As I argue in this paper, psychoanalysis is many different things, one of which is a scientific endeavour.

Many of the remaining papers are very much influenced by the work and thinking of Wilfred Bion.

'Freud's "selected fact": his journey of mourning', published in *the International Journal of Psycho-Analysis* follows.

'All the rage: Bion, psychic destructiveness, and the "death instinct"', is transcribed from a public lecture given on behalf of the Sydney Institute for Psychoanalysis. It considers Bion's early embracing of the idea of the death instinct, and his gradual movement away from this position.

'"Outside of time": free associations from the Antipodes' was published in the annual *Bulletin of the British Psychoanalytical Society*, Vol. 4 2014, as a cultural reflection on our situation 'Downunder'.

'"Think pig! Think": Beckett and Bion, *Waiting for Godot*' is a 'playful' consideration of the psychoanalytic parallels between the thinking of Samuel Beckett, and Wilfred Bion. This is followed by a poem *Encounter: Beckett/Bion,* published in the Irish literary magazine, *Crannog*.

There follow two philosophical papers on the mind/body or mind/brain problem published in *The Australia and New Zealand Journal of Psychiatry* in 2001.

The collection ends with A Tribute to Neville Symington.

An elegy for mourning and 'subjecticide'

In my side vision a small bird glimpsed, flying towards the car, disappears from view… reappears, tumbling up over the bonnet. Suspended, for a moment it seems, in front of our eyes; strangely folded upon itself, the breast feathers pale, the back darker. I think I see two trailing legs, impossibly thin, and then it is gone, sucked up and away, a tiny feathered packet of shattered bones, to find its resting place, somewhere on the roadside just outside the town of Puéchabon in Rousillon, France.

'Couldn't you have avoided it?' My wife putting into words my own fantasy; going back in time, replaying the events with a different outcome. For a moment it seems inconceivable, as though it couldn't have happened, perhaps it hadn't; no impact had been heard or felt, perhaps the bird was not dead at all…? But of course, it had happened, and the bird's life was certainly extinguished. Could I have avoided it? The whole event was over in perhaps a second, the bird's fate sealed in the trajectory of its flight and that of our travel.

I wanted to blame the car. It wasn't the small vehicle that we had requested. The hire company had 'upgraded' us to the only vehicle they had left: big, black, ruthless, a computer on wheels, like some kind of twenty-first century 'rough beast'. But no, it wasn't the machine itself, rather the 'ghost in the machine' who must take responsibility, who made the decisions and took the steps, that had sealed the fate of the little bird. Mercifully the driver, the ghost in the machine, has not yet been made redundant….

I drove on, surprised by a profound sense of sadness and loss. The acute feeling soon passed, but all that day, and into the night the image of the broken bird seemed to hang somewhere in my mind, not far away, demanding a response. Why was I so affected? There was, of course, the extreme vulnerability of the bird, and then it seemed such a long time since I had killed a bird while driving. I thought back to my own country forty years ago; there were so many birds that their random killing was an inevitable consequence of driving; a certain amount of slaughter was the accepted price that had to be paid. Life entails the inevitability of death; was this all to do with my own growing older? The nearer we approach the end, the more insistent we may feel its presence. It seems there often comes a point in life at which we begin to live with this consciousness ever present in the back of our mind; living in the shadow of death creates both a new poignancy in life, and a new urgency to live.

Perhaps this sense of loss was sharpened by the fact we were returning from a walk in the countryside of Rousillon, where we had remarked how few birds there seemed to be. I thought of the ruthless exploitation of migratory birds in the Mediterranean countries for food. In his 2010 essay 'The Ugly Mediterranean', Jonathan Franzen documents how in the mid-1990s, two decades after songbird trapping had been outlawed in Cyprus, 'as many as ten million songbirds a year were being killed. To meet the restaurant demand, traditional lime-stick trapping had been augmented by large-scale netting operations.' Then the Cypriot government, 'which was trying to clean up its act and win entry in the European Union, cracked down hard on netters. By 2006 the annual take had fallen to around a million' (Franzen, 2010 p. 79). However, 'In the past few years ... with Cyprus now comfortably ensconced in the EU ... the number of active trapping sites is rising' (ibid. p. 80). The results of lime-sticking and netting are evoked painfully in Franzen's description of entering what might be described as a war zone, where members of the organization 'The Committee Against Bird Slaughter' attempt, at considerable risk to themselves, to disrupt and sabotage these illegal activities; activities that would seem to serve a collective greed and macho pride. As Franzen discovers, the violence is not just for the birds. Some sins certainly are deadly.

As the course and reality of the First World War unfolded, Sigmund Freud was forced to recognize the presence of a delusional state within his mind. In 'The Disillusionment of War', one of two linked essays published as 'Thoughts for the Time on War and Death' (Freud, 1915), Freud documented his belief before the coming war that this would proceed as a 'chivalrous passage of arms, which would limit itself to establishing superiority of one side in the struggle, while as far as possible avoiding acute suffering that could contribute nothing to the decision, and granting complete immunity for the wounded…' and so on. 'There would, of course, be the utmost consideration for the non-combatant classes…' but, 'Then the war in which we refused to believe broke out, and it brought—disillusionment. Not only is it more bloody and destructive than any war of other days… it is at least as cruel, as embittered, as implacable as any that has preceded it.' (ibid. p. 278).

Freud recognized he had been under the sway of wish fulfilment and an 'illusion' about the human potential for violence and destructiveness. He concedes that if we embrace illusions in order to spare ourselves 'unpleasurable feelings', then we 'must not complain… if now and again they come into collision with some portion of reality, and are shattered against it' (ibid. p. 280). In 'Our Attitude Towards Death', the companion piece in 'Thoughts for the Time on War and Death' (1915), Freud suggests there is a gain in 'having to confront the reality of death, and giving death its due also helps us to escape from illusion, and therefore allows a fuller appreciation of the value of life.' In his essay 'On Transience', Freud creates the impression that his companion, a young poet, is in a melancholic state of mind, and conjectures there must have been some powerful emotional factor disturbing the judgment of the poet and his friend. He concludes, 'What spoilt their enjoyment of beauty must have been a revolt in their minds against mourning.' (Freud, 1916 p. 306)

He suggests transience can only increase the value of what is beautiful: 'A flower that blooms only for a single night does not seem to us on that account any less lovely' (ibid. p. 305).

Freud was soon to publish perhaps his most penetrating text of all, 'Mourning and Melancholia' (1917), written mostly in 1915. In it he considers the similarities and overlap of the pictures of states of mourning and states of melancholia. He observes that melancholic states are accompanied by a critical, even violent attitude towards the self, a feature absent in mourning. He explores the nature and origin of these destructive elements in melancholia, and makes the point that melancholia is like a derailed mourning where the awareness of what has been lost is withdrawn from consciousness.

Mourning, by contrast, is a fully conscious experience depending upon the awareness of what has been lost. Mourning is a painful process that follows its own course and, if followed to completion, results in a restoration of the good, and restoration of the capacity to love. If there is no awareness of what has been lost, mourning is not possible, but without mourning there is no restoration or renewal.

The absence of mourning leaves us in a ruthless and depleted world; a melancholic, pre-ruth world. But the capacity to experience loss and to mourn is a complex and fragile one, dependent upon an appreciation of realities; in particular the awareness of loss and limitation, the reality of death, and the awareness of our own destructiveness. Unless we recognize and feel the loss of the bird populations of Europe, effective action to restore what has been lost would seem unlikely. Here in Australia, if we do not collectively recognize the realities of global warming, deforestation, ocean pollution and species loss, whether on land or in the sea, then mourning for a damaged environment cannot take place, and effective redress is unlikely.

Our post-modern world, however, would seem in danger of lurching into a post-mourning world. Are we collectively destroying and losing the capacity to mourn? Are we now faced with the need to mourn the loss of the capacity for mourning? It is a fraught endeavour to attempt to characterize and predict social currents, but increasingly we live in an operationalized world, where outcomes and the 'deal' trumps any appreciation of reality and truth. A 'be happy' world where nothing is lost and consequently there is nothing to mourn.

Psychoanalyst Christopher Bollas has suggested the existence of a collective psychic trend in Western culture towards the destruction of personhood, including the capacity to think, feel, and register the pain of the human condition. For this state of mind, he has coined the term 'subjecticide'.

Bollas's thesis is that violence that is not directed physically towards the person, as suicide or homicide, may be redirected towards wiping out personal subjectivity. He suggests we appear to be gradually slipping away from negotiating our realities, and accepting 'a selective perception of the world that is turning negative hallucination into an art form" (Bollas, 2015 p. 538). In contrast to the hallucination, the perception of something that is not there, the psychoanalytic concept of a 'negative hallucination' refers to the denial in perception of what actually is there. Bollas's term subjecticide, with its suggestion of being a suicide equivalent, captures the real violence involved in the attack upon truth and the perception of reality.

Good literature has always been and always will be about enhancing the appreciation of reality, of what is there, and from this perspective fosters the development of the capacity to mourn what has been lost. Mourning is the very heart of poetry in particular; the manifest theme of Samuel Taylor Coleridge's *The Rime of the Ancient Mariner*, is destruction of the albatross, loss, depression and mourning. Or consider John Keats's *When I have fears I may cease to be*:

And when I feel, fair creature of an hour,
That I shall never look upon thee more,
Never have relish in the faery power
Of unreflecting love—then on the shore
Of the wide world I stand alone, and think
Till love and fame to nothingness do sink.

Statistically, we are informed, the global citizen is less likely to meet a violent death than at any time in the historical past. Encouraging no doubt, but not, I believe, grounds for optimism. Violence towards truth is a necessary precondition for the outbreak of mass murder and collective violence that the world witnessed in the holocaust, and there seems little to suggest that the assault on truth is any less potent or pervasive today. If Bollas's analysis is correct—that both homicide and suicide, which psychoanalytically we recognize as the inverse of one another, are becoming further transformed into a third possibility: subjecticide—then the assault on truth may be more, rather than less, pervasive.

In the twenty-first century the focus of the psychoanalytic endeavour has become the pursuit of truth, with the necessary qualification that truth is always multifaceted and often extremely difficult to discern. Truth is apprehended through exploration of our individual capacity to deny or modify what is true. Elusive as 'the truth' may prove to be, nevertheless the pursuit of truth can often be sharply distinguished from violence towards the truth, the pursuit of lies and 'fake news'. Psychoanalysis, environmental activism, literary creativity, and all truly artistic, scientific, and humanitarian activities, lend weight to the recognition of reality, the pursuit of truth, and development of the capacity to mourn. They may or may not be enough, but they are all that we have to stave off subjecticide, and our collective capacity for self-destruction.

References

Bollas, C. (2015). Psychoanalysis in the age of bewilderment: On the return of the oppressed. *The International Journal of Psychoanalysis* 96(3):35–551.

Franzen, J. (2010). The Ugly Mediterranean. Reprinted in J. Franzen (2012). *Farther Away*. London: Fourth Estate.

Freud, S. (1915). Thoughts for the time on war and death. In J. Strachey (Ed. & Trans.). *The Standard Edition of the Complete Psychological Works of Sigmund Freud* (Vol. 14).

——— (1916). On transience. In J. Strachey (Ed. & Trans.). *The Standard Edition of the Complete Psychological Works of Sigmund Freud* (Vol. 14).

——— (1917). Mourning and melancholia. In J. Strachey (Ed. & Trans.). *The Standard Edition of the Complete Psychological Works of Sigmund Freud* (Vol. 14).

Medicine and the manic defence

Published in *The Australian* and *New Zealand Journal of Psychiatry*, 1998, 32(3):392–397

This paper reflects upon the propensity of medical practitioners to intervene by active 'doing' when faced with presentations of a psychosomatic or psychological nature, and suggests that such intervention often manifests the unconscious operation of a manic defence. Manic defences militate against the recognition of complex clinical realities of a psychological nature, and hence against the development of psychotherapeutic skills to accommodate those realities. Within this context an understanding of the psychological forces that influence current approaches to the treatment of depression is offered.

The manic defence as defined by Melanie Klein is characterized by denial and omnipotence, disparagement, control, and idealization (Klein,1940). Developmentally, manic defences are thought to arise from the infant's attempts to maintain an illusion of omnipotence and control in the face of threatening experiences of vulnerability and frustration.

The inevitable reality of infantile frustration also provides a stimulus towards integration of the self and the achievement of the 'depressive position' (ibid.), or in Winnicott's terminology, the development of the 'capacity for concern' (Winnicott 1944). Frustration gives rise to aggressive impulses and fantasies of harm to the object, which lead in turn to anxiety, primitive guilt, and the wish for reparation; the beginning of the 'capacity for concern'. In the normal course of events, as the depressive position is consolidated, manic defences lessen; the mother is recognized as separate and not under omnipotent control, and the child develops a realistic acceptance of his dependence, and of his own ambivalence. However, even in favourable developmental circumstances, Klein (1940) felt the propensity to enact a manic defence is never completely transcended, and remains in some degree common to everyone. She regarded such enactments as everyday phenomena.

While depressive anxieties, guilt, and reparative wishes lead the way out of infantile omnipotence, this is a gradual process. Early or 'primitive' reparative fantasies incorporate elements of omnipotence and denial, and may possess a quality of compulsion. Klein formulated the concept of 'manic reparation' to describe the situation where attempts at reparation become, and remain, fused with elements of infantile omnipotence.

Manic reparation manifests as a compulsive need to put things right, and a propensity to react, rather than to reflect and respond. Such 'reactive' doing serves to avoid realities: both the real complexities and difficulties of a situation, and the feelings of doubt and uncertainty, the 'depressive anxieties', engendered by it. Hinshelwood (1989) states that where manic reparation is activated, 'the whole situation has to be belittled and the task made light of as if it can be accomplished by magic.' Segal (1988) emphasizes that when a person establishes a pattern of manic reparation this tends to be carried out in relation to remote objects/persons for which the individual has no prior responsibility, thus the potential satisfactions of the reparative act are experienced free from a sense of guilt about the object as damaged by the self. Such reparation brings no lasting satisfaction, however, and must be carried out over and over.

Manic reparation is more than the expression of a wish to cure; it is driven by a need to cure. In his now classic 1957 paper 'The Ailment', Tom Main reflected upon the doctor's investment in, and need to cure:

> The best kind of patient for this purpose is one who from great suffering and danger of life or sanity responds quickly to a treatment that interests his doctor and thereafter remains completely well; but those who recover only slowly or incompletely are less satisfying. Only the most mature of therapists are able to encounter frustration of their hopes without some ambivalence towards the patient, and with patients who do not get better, or who even get worse in spite of long devoted care, major strain may arise. The patient's attendants are then pleased neither with him nor themselves and the quality of their concern alters accordingly, with consequences that can be severe both for patients and attendants.

Physical medicine

The doctor's need to intervene actively may serve well in the treatment of organic illness, which appropriately involves active physical interventions applied to ameliorate a disorder or its symptoms. However, in physical medicine, and especially in general practice, the doctor encounters patients whose somatic presentations are determined by underlying psychological disorder. Michael Balint, in his 1986 book *The Doctor, his Patient and the Illness,* provides a wealth of clinical case material drawn from experience supervising small groups of general practitioners, in order to illustrate the complexities of psychosomatic presentations. In these 'Balint Groups', he attempted to facilitate the diagnostic formulation of such patients, and to show how apparently organically determined symptoms often proved significantly psychogenic in origin, if the practitioner was prepared to undertake a fuller assessment. In such cases, the physical diagnosis proposed by the general practitioner was usually a descriptive label, without etiological explanatory power. A prerequisite for rational treatment was a 'deeper diagnosis' that included a tentative etiological formulation taking into account the psychological and emotional forces at work.

Often the general practitioner's training does not provide a framework of knowledge adequate to the interpretation of complex phenomena with psychosocial dimensions. The doctor's ability to formulate such phenomena will also depend upon personal capacities of psychological and emotional understanding. To avoid potential experiences of uncertainty, vulnerability, or impotence, the doctor may unconsciously restrict his inquiry to familiar areas, and a physical diagnosis provides the opportunity to offer some tangible physical treatment or investigation. Such 'doing' contains elements of a manic defence, creating an illusion of control and omnipotence, and engendering an attitude of idealization on the part of the patient.

In contrast to physical therapies, treatment effects that are psychotherapeutic often depend not upon active doing, but upon containment of the patient's anxiety in order that exploration and acknowledgement of relevant emotional and interpersonal issues can take place. As Balint's case material demonstrates, it is this very process of acknowledgement, exploration, and understanding, that often constitutes the needed treatment. The psychological understanding gained also helps avoid unnecessary physical investigation and treatment.

Psychological medicine

The psychiatrist is the medical practitioner who might be expected to possess the skills to achieve greater integration in the understanding of mind and body. It is my contention, however, that—despite their training, or perhaps to some extent because of it—psychiatrists collectively remain prone to invoking inappropriately concrete conceptual structures in the face of the complexities of the psychological (Ross and Pam, 1995), and tend to a manic defence in prescribing treatment. History reveals this tendency in the pattern of adoption of new physical treatments in psychiatry during this century. Insulin coma therapy enjoyed a period of considerable popularity, and psychiatrists were quick to take up the new treatment of psychosurgery, which was extensively employed beyond the boundaries of any established efficacy (Clare,1976). The advent of electroconvulsive therapy (ECT) was followed by a similar pattern of uncritical acceptance and application (Clare, 1976). Many patients suffered as a consequence of their psychiatrists' therapeutic zeal.

Janet Frame, the well-known New Zealand novelist[1], spent lengthy admissions in several of her country's psychiatric institutions between 1945 and 1954, receiving, in the course of this treatment, a diagnosis of schizophrenia. Frame's novel *Faces in the Water* (1961) offers an evocative subjective response to these experiences. Her 1989 autobiography devotes relatively few pages to this period of her life, but what she does say leaves the reader in no doubt about the nature of her experience, nor is it possible to seriously doubt that her 'treatment' was inappropriate and abusive:

> I was discharged from hospital 'on probation'. After having received over two hundred applications of unmodified E.C.T., each the equivalent, in degree of fear, to an execution, and in the process having my memory shredded and in some aspects weakened permanently or destroyed, and after having been subjected to proposals to have myself changed, by a physical operation, into a more acceptable, amenable, normal person, I arrived home at Willowglen, outwardly smiling and calm, but inwardly with all confidence gone, with the

1 Reader's outside New Zealand may be aware of the film *An Angel at my Table*, based upon Frame's autobiographical writings.

> conviction at last that I was officially a non-person. I had seen enough of schizophrenia to know that I had never suffered from it.

Frame was saved from being subjected to a leucotomy for her 'schizophrenia' in a last-minute reversal of her doctor's orders as a fortuitous result of his learning that she had received a literary prize for her first published book of short stories.

Contemporary psychiatry in Australia and New Zealand is much changed since Frame's experience. Treatments are more thoroughly researched and psychiatrists have better training, but these factors alone cannot ensure that practitioners acquire deeper psychological understanding. Human nature does not change so readily or comprehensively. To the extent that psychiatry continues to manifest a collective, and to some extent institutionalized, preference for doing to, rather than being with, the patient, the focus for 'doing' has shifted to the prescribing of psychotropic drugs. The phenomenon of the uncritical application of new treatments seems to be being repeated in the current wave of prescribing of antidepressant medications.

Treatment of depression

The pervasive focus on biological research in academic psychiatry has recently attracted trenchant criticism (Ross and Pam, 1995), in particular the failure of 'bioreductionist' models, as they have been labelled by their detractors, to give serious consideration to psychological and social factors in the etiology of 'functional' psychiatric disorders. The present discussion in relation to depression assumes the etiological importance of psychological and interpersonal factors, and suggests that prevalent treatment approaches manifest this bioreductionist tendency in their failure to adequately address these factors. Such treatment approaches are conceptualized as enactments of a manic defence. Although depression is taken as an example, analogous arguments could be put forward in relation to the treatment of a variety of disorders of complex etiology.

Antidepressant medications can have a role in the treatment of depression, but the reassurance of the promised 'cure' can also contribute to an avoidance of the necessary exploration of relevant emotional and psychological processes. As symptoms of depression usually (but not always) represent a manifestation, or aspect, of specific dynamic processes within the mind of the patient of which the patient is not fully aware, medicative treatment prescribed to treat symptoms without elucidation of the meaning of the depression, is equivalent to treatment before diagnostic formulation.

Prescribing can be a manifestation of the practitioner's defensive need either to avoid recognition of the complexity of the presenting complaint, or to maintain distance from the patient's experience of psychic pain. Prescribing on such a basis will be welcome to the patient if it mirrors his wish to avoid or deny deeper psychological realities. Alternatively, the patient may experience a failure of empathic understanding, reflecting the psychiatrist's wish to treat the symptom experienced rather than the self experiencing.

When apparent benefit ensues from a course of antidepressant medication, the hope of a quick and complete 'cure', whether held by patient or practitioner, usually proves illusory. If treatment has been initiated on a defensive basis, and a satisfactory outcome is not achieved, the resultant anxiety may be manifest in an inflexible pursuit of further medicative treatment. Patients can become involved in lengthy processes of medication adjustment and combination, without concurrent attempts to understand the possible psychological meaning of symptoms, or to embark on treatment which might address such issues.

In a 1996 address to the Royal Australian and New Zealand College of Psychiatry (RANZCP), later published in the college's journal, *Australasian*

Psychiatry (1997), New Zealand Mental Health Commissioner Julie Leibrich described her personal experiences of treatment for depression:

> For about 4 years I had a variety of treatments, but the focus was always drug therapy: drugs, drugs, and more drugs. I put on weight. I couldn't drive a car. I couldn't swallow properly. I was walking dead. I experienced humiliation after humiliation yet *drugs did not take away the pain, only my ability to learn from it.* (Italics added)

It is a frequent story from patients who find their way into therapy. Even if the apparent side effects described here would be lessened with newer drugs, I think the last sentence in Leibrich's statement captures the essential limitation of biological treatments for many depressed patients. The treatment approach described can develop in ways that are harmful to the patient. In Main's words, 'The sufferer who frustrates a keen therapist by failing to improve is always in danger of meeting primitive human behaviour disguised as treatment' (Main, 1957).

Main reminds us of our human capacity to enact the frustration consequent upon our failures.

Freud first formulated the concept of countertransference in recognition of his own capacity to enact unconscious conflicts in relation to the patient. As Gabbard (1997) has remarked, 'the very difficulty in knowing about countertransference is the fact that it is unconscious, we therefore tend to become aware of it through our actions.' Because physical treatments can be offered immediately, tangibly, and actively, they carry a reassurance that other treatments may not, and can be readily employed as part of the enactment of a manic defence by therapist, patient, or both.

However, psychological therapies can also serve as vehicles for enactment, and any psychological therapy can potentially be utilized in a reductionist way that militates against recognition of psychological complexity. Cognitive and behavioural therapies, which provide structured approaches and limit the scope of psychological inquiry, perhaps most readily lend themselves to employment in this manner. While cognitive-behavioural therapies have importance, the current advocacy of the application of these treatments according to protocols for a range of disorders, including depression, might be interpreted as the collective enactment of an unconscious wish to limit the scope of psychological inquiry and treatment to the realms of cognition and/or behaviour, in order to avoid the 'depressive anxieties' inherent in incorporating the patient's emotional experience and the therapist's response to it.

When Freud (1957) recognized the connection between normal mourning and pathological melancholia, he also recognized that melancholia is distinguished from mourning by an active process of self-directed aggression. In certain kinds of melancholia (Freud was careful to emphasize that clinical depression may have varying etiologies) 'we see that the ego debases itself and rages against itself.' Despite subsequent developments of theory, Freud's insight remains central to the dynamic conceptualization of depression. Full psychological understanding of depression must include recognition of this process of self-directed aggression or hatred, and recognition that the depression itself represents a kind of defence against the turning outward of such 'hostility'. Such understanding, if accepted, raises the possibility that the evocation of a manic defence in prescribing treatment for depression represents a defence against recognition of destructive forces within the patient. Possibly the need to defend against such recognition is greatest when the practitioner is unable to recognize the existence of such forces within himself.

Psychiatrists and psychotherapists often function as idealized transference figures for patients, or in self-psychological terms, they provide an idealized self-object function. Whatever the theoretical background of the practitioner, clinical psychotherapeutic experience inevitably creates awareness of the negative transferences that tend to underlie a patient's idealisation. If dependence and idealization have been allowed to evolve naturally in the transference, and a robust treatment alliance is established, then the working through of the negative transference, the 'hostility', is usually possible as this becomes manifest in response to the inevitable frustrations of the psychotherapeutic process. If however the idealising function becomes located in the psychiatrist as the prescriber of antidepressant medications, or even in the medications themselves in their transitional object function, and the nature of the treatment alliance does not allow for the exploration of such emotional investments then, I believe, the process of treatment can easily develop in ways that are countertherapeutic. Even when a patient experiences symptomatic improvement as a result of medicative treatment, he may nevertheless be denied the opportunity to work through conflicts determining the symptomatic presentation, and the long-term risk of relapse may not be altered.

Discussion

Psychiatric symptoms are often regarded by the psychiatrist in the same way physical symptoms were often regarded by Balint's general practitioners: as the end point of inquiry. Treatment is then instituted as a protocol according to a symptom-based diagnosis, and there may be little or no attempt to consider the possible meaning of symptoms, or to search for the 'deeper diagnosis'. While this is sometimes appropriate, it is not always so.

I have suggested that such an approach to treatment is determined not only by limitations of training and knowledge, but also by the operation of a manic defence. The need to cure contains elements of manic reparation, and the manic defence requires maintenance of certainty and closure. Thus, the patient's disorder must be reduced to a complexity commensurate with the therapeutic conceptions and techniques of the doctor.

The operation of the manic defence is to some extent institutionalized in medicine, and a medical training can be employed to promote a defensive medicalisation of the vagaries of human experience; a situation which militates against the acquisition of psychotherapeutic skills. However, such a state of affairs is not inherent in the phenomenological and analytic approach of the medical model itself. The psychoanalytic method began as Freud's attempt to apply this analytic diagnostic approach to the complexity of mental phenomena as the basis of a scientific psychology. The ability to bring this essentially scientific analytic capacity to clinical work constitutes one of the essential attributes for effective psychotherapeutic function.

The psychoanalyst D.W. Winnicott (1944) was able to use his medical training, and experience as a pediatrician, to great advantage as a psychotherapist, but was acutely aware that the physician's need to cure can lead to difficulties in the face of psychological disorder. In his paper on the presentation of symptoms relating to the eye in children, he wrote:

> I am half afraid to describe psychological matters to an audience of doctors. Doctors seem to have to treat and cure every symptom. But in psychology this is a snare and a delusion. One must be able to note symptoms without trying to cure them because every symptom has its value to the patient, and very frequently the patient is better left with his symptom. *In any case one must be able to describe psychological matters without immediately having to answer the question as to how to cure what is described.* (Italics added)

The reactive need to 'cure' to the extent that it pre-empts reflection and understanding, is the essence of the manic defence in medicine.

Most of us come to medicine with a need to cure fused with a degree of grandiose ambition. As Main (1957) has pointed out we enter medicine for deep personal reasons, and the practice of medicine has abiding, unconscious determinants. The psychiatrist's treatment, like the treatment of any doctor, will be influenced by his or her unconscious wishes, and a doctor's capacity for insight into the minds of his patients invariably depends upon his capacity for insight into his own.

References

Balint, M. (1986). *The Doctor, His Patient and the Illness.* Edinburgh: Churchill Livingston.

Clare, A. (1976). *Psychiatry in Dissent: Controversial Issues in Thought and Practice.* London: Tavistock Publications.

Frame, J. (1961). *Faces in the Water.* Christchurch: Pegasus Press.

——— (1989). *An Autobiography.* Auckland: Century Hutchinson New Zealand.

Freud, S. (1957). Mourning and melancholia. In J. Strachey (Ed. & Trans.). *The Standard Edition of the Complete Psychological Works of Sigmund Freud* (Vol. 14, pp. 237–258). London: Hogarth Press.

Gabbard, G.O. (1997). Lessons to be learned from the study of sexual boundary violations. *Australian and New Zealand Journal of Psychiatry* 31:321–327.

Hinshelwood, R.D. (1989). *A Dictionary of Kleinian Thought.* London: Free Association Books.

Klein M. (1940). Mourning and its relation to manic-depressive states. *International Journal of Psycho-Analysis* 21:125–153.

Leibrich, J. (1997). The doors of perception. *Australian and New Zealand Journal of Psychiatry* 31:36–45.

Main, T.F. (1957). The ailment. *British Journal of Medical Psychology* 30:129–145.

Ross C, Pam A. (1995). *Pseudoscience in Biological Psychiatry: Blaming the Body.* New York: John Wiley and Sons.

Segal, H. (1988). Reparation. In *Introduction to the Work of Melanie Klein* (pp. 92–102). London: Karnac.

Winnicott, D.W. (1944). Ocular psychoneuroses of childhood. In *Through Paediatrics to Psychoanalysis: Collected Papers*. London: Karnac.

——— (1990). The development of the capacity for concern. In *The Maturational Processes and the Facilitating Environment.* London: Karnac.

Psychoanalysis: what is it and why is it hated?

This paper was previously published in *The Australasian Journal of Psychotherapy*, Vol. 28, 1 & 2, 2009

Abstract

Psychoanalysis is considered to be the activity of investigation of the mind for the purpose of delineating personal psychic truth. Insofar as the aim of psychoanalysis is the pursuit of truth, it is considered to be a science. The relationship between psychoanalysis and psychotherapy is considered, as are certain elements of the psychoanalytic encounter. It is suggested that hatred of psychoanalysis will be encountered in all parties, consequent upon the inevitable presence within us of a hatred of, or resistance to, the delineation of psychic truth.

Psychic truth

In Shakespeare's *Hamlet* Polonius advises his son Laertes who is about to travel abroad:

> This above all—to thine own self be true,
> And it must follow, as the night the day,
> Thou canst not then be false to any man.' (Act 1, Sc 3)

The question of authenticity or being true to oneself is as fundamental to the human mind as Hamlet's question 'To be or not to be'. We might even suspect the two issues come down to much the same thing: that a false existence is just that, an existence, but no real life, no real being. The psychoanalyst Donald Winnicott (1960) proposed the idea of a 'false self', which arose as an adaptation to developmental experience that is not growth-promoting. He saw this false self as a way of staying in existence, of keeping alive the possibility that one day something of the authentic being within the person may be realized. Winnicott called this latent potential the 'true self'.

That Shakespeare gives Polonius wise words should give pause for thought, because Polonius 'was in life a foolish prating knave', as Hamlet comments, after he has mistaken Polonius, who is hiding behind a curtain, for his stepfather, and stabbed him to death (Act 3, Sc 4). It is a case of hidden and mistaken identity. Psychically Polonius's real self is in hiding; it has never come to life. He is the stepfather or false father of the mind. Without a mind of his own, his identity is a false one, so he bends like a reed in the wind with the prevailing opinion:

> Hamlet: Do you see yonder cloud that's almost in shape of a camel?
> Polonius: By the mass, and 'tis like a camel, indeed.
> Hamlet: Methinks it is like a weasel.
> Polonius: It is backed like a weasel.
> Hamlet: Or like a whale.
> Polonius: Very like a whale. (Act 3, Sc 2)

In giving Polonius the words 'To thine own self be true,' Shakespeare ironically draws attention to the fact that this task, of being true to oneself, is no easy one, as the self in question must be conceptualized as having not only conscious but also unconscious dimensions. If it is not to be avoided, the task will prove a lifetime's work. For some of us this work includes psychoanalysis and psychotherapy.

As he developed his psychoanalytic technique Freud (1895d) placed roughly equal emphases on the aims of treating the minds of his patients, and investigating the minds of his patients. Although the two may be difficult to separate, there is merit in considering the investigation of the mind as the primary aim of psychoanalysis. The reason being that optimal therapeutic effects are consequent upon true understanding, so the primary aim of clinical psychoanalysis can be considered that of understanding the mind of the analysand or patient. Paradoxically, therapeutic ambition, and in particular the desire to cure the patient of symptoms and suffering, tends to undermine the pursuit of understanding. Of necessity, the process of understanding comes first, and any inherent therapeutic effects are consequent. The curing of the mind, to the extent that this takes place, is a by-product of the activity of understanding.

Freud (1923a) came to define psychoanalysis as broadly covering three things. First, a procedure for the investigation of mental processes which are almost inaccessible in any other way; second, a method for the treatment of psychological disorders; and third, a body of theory accumulated into a scientific discipline. Just as the therapeutic effects of psychoanalysis follow from the process of investigation, so the accumulation of a body of scientific theory—Freud's third definition of psychoanalysis—is also secondary to the process of investigation. General theories can be hypothesized by induction from particular instances discovered in individual patients.

Clinical psychoanalysis then is an activity concerned primarily with investigation of the mind and the delineation of personal psychic truth.

In the collective Western psyche, the term psychoanalysis remains associated with Freud and his theories, and certain aspects of the psychoanalytic technique, such as the couch. But these objects, even the illustrious Freud himself, have no essential link to the concept of psychoanalysis under consideration. This psychoanalysis is not dependent upon any particular theory. It has nothing to do with the cult of personality, nothing to do with any particular 'school' of psychoanalysis, nor does it belong to any psychoanalytic institution. An understanding of this particular psychoanalysis is not dependent upon a psychoanalytic training, although good training can greatly promote it. It does not depend upon the title 'psychoanalyst'. It may or may not be present in a psychoanalyst, in a psychotherapist, or indeed within anybody. If it is to be located at all, it is identified in a psychoanalytic attitude—that is an attitude, inherently scientific, of observation and inquiry towards psychic reality. This attitude of wanting to get to know about something has been designated 'K' by the psychoanalyst Wilfred Bion (1962).

Although we think of Freud as the legitimate father of psychoanalysis, the psychoanalytic attitude that I am describing existed before Freud. In this sense there were 'psychoanalysts' before Freud, Shakespeare being one of the most notable. The literary critic Harold Bloom (1998) identifies Shakespeare's art of characterization, with its focus on the inner self, as something that was radically new. Bloom points out the sense of reality that attaches to Shakespeare's characters, something not achieved in the drama of his contemporaries.

As a further powerful example of Shakespeare's imaginative grasp of psychological truth consider his development of the character of Lear in *King Lear*. Through Lear, Shakespeare portrays the psychotic breakdown of the self, which leads ultimately to Lear's painful realization of his own foolishness and destructiveness, and to the beginning emergence of a new and more integrated self. In the first scene of the play, Regan comments of her father: '...he hath ever but slenderly known himself' (Act 1, Sc 1). Lear's tragedy is that self-knowledge comes at the end of his life, but nevertheless self-knowledge is affirmed as possible.

It is an observable clinical fact that some patients emerge from states of emotional breakdown and psychosis having attained a greater degree of psychological integration than previously, and a process of self-discovery is often initiated by the breakdown of the existing structure of the personality. In such cases it is difficult to avoid the impression that it would have been impossible for the patient to gain his or her own mind without first losing it. It is very striking that Shakespeare possessed such a clear intuitive understanding of the potential therapeutic value of psychological breakdown. It is also striking that this phenomenon is largely ignored by contemporary psychiatry. The attitude of contemporary psychiatry towards this clinical fact is very much like Lear's attitude towards his daughter Cordelia: disinherited and banished because she does not conform to the dominant paradigm.

Harold Bloom (1998) titled his book on Shakespeare's plays *The Invention of the Human*. Bloom argues that the invention of what we call 'personality', and the modern conception of the self as a moral agent, really began with Shakespeare, who became, and has remained, an important force shaping the Western psyche. Bloom's use of the word 'invention' is not to be understood as suggesting something arbitrary, but rather as suggesting the realization of a potential. He writes: 'Our ideas as to what makes the self *authentically* human owe more to Shakespeare than ought to be possible' (p. 17, italics added).

Psychoanalysis as science

While psychoanalysis is many things, it is a scientific undertaking. The philosopher Collingwood (1940 p. 4) has defined science as 'systematic or orderly thinking about a determinate subject matter.' One necessary element of a science is that it attempts to approach the 'truth' about the phenomena toward which it directs its attention. It tends to try to find out about these phenomena.

It follows that psychoanalysis, in order to try and delineate this object called 'psychic truth,' adopts an essentially scientific stance. It is the natural science of the psyche or mind.

Obviously, words like 'truth' have to be used with some care. It is used here in the sense suggested by Bion, as something that, like Kant's (1783) noumenon, exists, but which we cannot know directly. Bion (1970) calls this truth or existence 'ultimate reality'. In brief he suggests we approach knowledge of 'ultimate reality' indirectly through the process he calls 'K'—that is the attempt to get to know about something. Through K we gain knowledge of the phenomena of existence, and form mental representations or theories about ultimate reality, which however we cannot know directly.

A science is identified primarily on the basis of the kind of phenomena towards which it directs attention, rather than on the basis of specific current theories. To some extent theories come and go in all sciences. Given the interpretive nature of psychoanalysis, and the fact that it deals with ineffable subjective realities, it is particularly prone to the proliferation of theories. So, psychoanalysis may generate theories but it is not defined by current theories.

To relegate theory to a secondary role is not to suggest that all theories of the mind are of equal value, so that it does not matter what theory we hold. It is, however, to suggest that in psychoanalysis, as in all science, investment in and adherence to a particular theory, or school of thinking, is likely to restrict one's capacity for observation. In the clinical context, faced with the immediacy and complexity of the psychoanalytic or psychotherapeutic encounter, when one person is trying to find out something about another, then any attempt to impose a theory or work from a theory restricts vision and experience, and if experience is restricted so is the data available to the analyst.

The analyst in the session is in the position of the scientist trying to make sense of a mass of data. What is unusual about the psychoanalyst's position, and which is perhaps rather different from the usual conception of the scientist, is that the analyst-therapist's data is the emotional experience of the session and associated thoughts. The analyst-therapist's subjective experience of participation in the emotional relationship with the patient is an essential part of the data.

The state of mind on which the analytic work depends is one conducive to something being realized or understood. Freud (1912e p. 112) characterized this state of mind as one of listening with evenly suspended attention, and Bion (1962 p. 36) referred to it as a state of 'reverie'. The analyst's reverie is a state of mind receptive to the experience of being with the other person/s, and conducive to the apprehension of links between the elements of this experience. When the links between elements are apprehended there is a further experience, that of things coming together in a meaningful way; of coherence. In the session this might be the experience of apprehending a meaningful connection between a number of elements in the patient's material that the analyst had not previously related together; Bion's (1962 p. 72) conception of the 'selected fact'. Of course, any such understanding, is in the nature of a provisional hypothesis which is then tested against the evolving direction and material of the session.

The task in the session is to come to an understanding which is relevant to the patient. The circumstances of the session can never be reproduced, and the experience is specific to analyst and patient. The problem with psychoanalytic investigation is that phenomena of interest exist only within the consulting room. Some attempt, more or less convincing, may be made to communicate about the events of a session to a third party, but the events themselves can never be reproduced.

Psychoanalysis as therapy

The psychoanalyst's consultation proceeds with the specific aim of fostering a psychoanalytic and psychotherapeutic process. Or at least this is what we might expect, but of course whether or not this is so ultimately depends on the person of the psychoanalyst. Similarly, this process may be fostered by the psychotherapist in his consulting room, but again this will depend upon his conception of what constitutes therapy.

It is necessary to consider the relationship of the terms psychoanalysis and psychotherapy. Some, or perhaps most, of the people we see have some sort of idea that they have a problem and an expectation of treatment of some kind. They quite reasonably think they are coming for therapy. There is, I believe, no doubt that psychoanalysis is potentially a most potent form of psychotherapy, the reason being that the mind, as Bion has suggested, grows through the apprehension of psychic truth. Truth is food for the development of the mind. Bion's (1962) model here is the nursing mother and baby. The mother, through her activity of reverie and response, provides food for the developing mind in a manner analogous to her provision of milk for the infant's developing body. In the absence of reverie, a mind develops in which emotional experience and thinking are compromised or absent.

I would therefore suggest that psychotherapeutic efficacy in general depends upon psychoanalytic efficacy. Effective psychotherapy as a sustained process, depends on the presence of a psychoanalytic function, as defined, and this psychoanalytic function is in fact *the* essential psychotherapeutic element.

At this point we must consider the paradox already alluded to: therapeutic ambition, that is the desire to cure the patient of symptoms and suffering, tends to undermine the pursuit of understanding. While the patient comes expecting some form of treatment, any investment on the part of the analyst-therapist in the therapeutic outcome is likely to distort his psychoanalytic function. Such a wish distorts the psychoanalytic lens.

Bion (1970 p. 56) puts it thus: 'it interferes with analytic work to permit desires for the patient's cure, or well-being, or future to enter the mind. Such desires erode the analyst's power to analyse and lead to progressive deterioration of his intuition.'

The therapist whose wish to cure his patient intrudes into the session is not in a frame of mind conducive to analytic work. He or she might, for example, seek to read phenomena within the session as signs of progress or lack of progress, rather than remaining open to deeper meanings; or a vulnerable patient might intuit, and become constrained by, the therapist's hope for, or expectation of, improvement. A patient who is not free to be ill in the session is equally not free to be cured.

Similarly, an assumption on the therapist's part that the patient's symptoms and psychic suffering are a bad thing, would reflect a state of mind unsuited to analytic work. The analyst-therapist attempts to maintain a position of impartiality regarding any wish on the patient's behalf for relief from symptoms and suffering.

It is perhaps a critical point in our development as therapists when we come to understand that to resist our own or our patient's recognition of the reality and extent of his or her difficulty and disturbance, is to compromise true understanding, and to compromise true understanding is to compromise treatment. In other words, the state of mind suitable for analytic work, and hence suitable for psychotherapeutic work, is one where the investment is in truth rather than cure.

The psychoanalytic encounter

Whatever else it is, the psychoanalytic encounter is a human emotional experience. If, as has been suggested, psychoanalysis is inherent in the human condition, then any encounter between people may potentially realize elements of a psychoanalytic process, but again the psychoanalytic consultation is specifically designed to foster the expression of, and reflection upon, these psychoanalytic elements. The psychoanalyst's position in relation to this experience is that of participant observer.

The analyst is a participant in the emotional experience created by the coming together of two people. The encounter also proceeds, at least from the analyst's point of view, as an observational investigation; an attempt to get to know about something. As suggested, any therapeutic effect that flows from this might be thought of as a by-product of this process of getting to know. This process of getting to know begins afresh with each patient, and with each session. It is fostered if the analyst-therapist's mind can be freed from assumptions, and this includes attachment to theories.

The need to maintain an essentially disinterested position with regard to theories, the patient's and the therapist's wishes and so on, has been suggested. The concept of 'negative capability' is a rather popularized one in psychoanalytic literature at the present, but it is relevant and important. The expression is from the poet John Keats (quoted in Motion, 1997 p. 217), who wrote in a letter:

> At once it struck me what quality went to form a Man of Achievement especially in Literature and which Shakespeare possessed so enormously—I mean *Negative Capability*, that is when man is capable of being in uncertainties, Mysteries, doubts, without any irritable reaching after fact and reason.

Understanding, like poetry, cannot be forced; we must be willing to wait for it to come. Impatience within the analyst-therapist is not a frame of mind conducive to the evolution of a psychoanalytic process.

Bion (1970) has also characterized the frame of mind conducive to analytic work as one 'beyond memory and desire'.

These ideas may seem all very well, a sort of ideal, but of course in the immediacy of the psychoanalytic encounter there may be enormous emotional pressure from the patient, who, unlike the analyst, is free to express all feelings including impatience and aggression. Under such conditions the analyst's task is to, at least, 'survive' (Winnicott, 1971), and at best to retain some capacity to think under fire (Bion, 1974). Nor is there such a thing as an infallible psychoanalyst. The only instrument of observation the therapist or analyst has is his or her mind. If the mind is a perceiving lens it is also a distorting one. The reason personal analysis is so important in training is that it hopefully goes some way to lessening the distorting effect of the observing instrument. In *Second Thoughts* Bion (1967 p. 130) wrote:

> I have … learned that no amount of psycho-analysis can insure the psycho-analyst against distortion of his material although his distortions may become less crude than they were before he had been psycho-analysed.

Bion further comments (1967 p. 138) 'the psycho-analyst's work is lonely work, that the only companion he has is his patient and his patient is by definition unreliable.' The data of the psychoanalytic experience exist only in the consulting room. For this reason, it is extremely difficult for the analyst-therapist to communicate about what he does.

For this same reason, as Bion (1967 p. 138) also points out, reliance cannot be placed on 'hostile criticism'. He comments:

> ...the ineffable nature of psycho-analysis makes it unlikely that so-called impartial criticism has any value beyond serving as an indication of the climate of opinion in which the psycho-analyst works.

Hatred of psychoanalysis

The current climate of opinion is characterized by the tendency to idealize psychoanalysis on the one hand, or to denigrate it on the other. Idealization and denigration may be thought of as emotional responses that emerge in the absence of a real relationship and of real understanding.

Hatred can be thought of as the wish to obliterate the hated object, and denigration as a form of hatred. There may be a felt antipathy, or a less conscious dismissal or denial of the hated thing. Hatred may be expressed in extreme or subtle ways. Hatred of analysis may be found within the analyst-patient couple, or outside of it, within a group or the wider society.

An attitude of hatred towards analysis, whether conscious or unconscious, seems invariably to be found to exist within the patient. But why should the patient hate psychoanalysis, the procedure from which he or she presumably expects help of one form or another? One way of conceptualizing this is as hatred of the psychic pain attendant upon truth. We naturally withdraw our hand from a naked flame to avoid physical pain, and something similar may often take place in the mind in response to painful psychic reality; a psychic defence. If the patient has created a comforting delusion, the basis of the patient's hatred of the truth may be understood as a wish to avoid what is feared to be unbearable psychic pain. The arrogance and omnipotence sometimes manifest by a so-called 'narcissistic' patient offers an example of an organized defence against the recognition of psychic truth. In the therapy room, such arrogance and omnipotence invariably reveal themselves to be forms of psychic protection; a defence against awareness of a developmental experience in which the true self has gone unrecognized and unvalued.

To the extent that the patient's way of understanding and experiencing the world is based upon self-deception, the mind will resist knowledge of psychic truth. Such truth is felt to threaten the existing organization of the mind, and threaten the release of feared pain into consciousness.

However, clinical experience suggests a further dimension to the attitude of hatred towards psychoanalysis. It is an observable clinical fact that human beings have the capacity to render or maintain a variety of states of mind unconscious. Just as psychic pain can exist in unconscious forms, hostile states of mind: frustration, envy, anger, may exist in latent or repressed forms. In the facilitating, intense, and sometimes provocative atmosphere of the therapy relationship, resistance and repression may attenuate, and new links are formed. Hostile feelings, anger and rage, may emerge, or erupt violently into consciousness, sometimes directed towards the therapist who is felt to be frustrating and persecutory. Interpretation of the presence of such forces within the mind is often strongly resisted, especially if they are felt to be a source of shame, and the potential for the direct experience of anger and hostility within the transference is often feared and hated. At the extreme a patient may live in fear of a regressive return to an experience of infantile frustration and trauma, with the re-emergence of intense psychic pain, violent anger, or even psychotic fragmentation.

The psychic organization which consists of an unconsciously hostile attitude towards both awareness of, and the conscious experience of, painful and hostile emotional states, is perhaps another description of an envious state of mind. Symington (2007 p. 286) has described idealization as the first stage of envy, in recognition of the way an apparently positive attitude of idealization may conceal, and then reveal, a negative, denigrating and spoiling attitude in the course of a therapeutic analysis; a process perhaps also formulated in phrases such as the 'emergence of a negative transference'. The psychoanalytic concept of the 'bad object' would seem to be another formulation of the existence of a latent emotional experience involving potential aggression and hostility. The attitude of fear and hatred which maintains this experience in an unconscious form constitutes a particular obstacle to the unfolding of the psychotherapeutic process, and psychoanalytic understanding.

Fairbairn has argued that analytic technique can be conceptualized as designed to facilitate 'a release of repressed bad objects from the unconscious', but 'it is also fear of just such a release that characteristically drives the patient to seek analytical aid in the first instance'. The patient is troubled by the presence of the 'bad object' and holds a fantasy that the idealized therapist will relieve him of it, whereas the actual process of therapeutic analysis will introduce him to it in one way or another. So, adds Fairbairn, 'It is only when the released bad objects are beginning to lose their terror for him that he really begins to appreciate the virtues of mental immunization therapy.' (1943 p. 75)

And why should the analyst hate psychoanalysis? Because the analyst too is only human; perhaps sometimes the process seems too difficult for the analyst as well as the patient, perhaps he is tired, or perhaps she is worried about some other external concern. But more importantly the analyst also resists certain truths and the work of analysis remains a potential challenge to the analyst's assumptions, delusions, and repudiated psychic reality. The analyst must also remain a patient if the work is to proceed.

The collective antipathy towards psychoanalysis sometimes encountered within groups, or within society, may reflect the collective resistances of the individuals within that group, but can also be understood as following from the fact that truth is subversive to the conventions of the group. That is to say, the conventions of the group may be expected to reflect an investment in ensuring the survival of the group, rather than an investment in truth. The perspective of psychoanalysis offered here favours independence of thought, and as such represents a threat to the establishment mentality of the group. This will be the case even when the group is a psychoanalytic or psychotherapy training institution.

For all his outward conventionality, Freud did not flinch from the recognition that conformity with any of society's codes of conduct and conventions was no measure of mental well-being; evidence as to the emotional health of a person had to be sought within. Freud was well aware of what Winnicott later came to call the 'false self'. Freud's position is, of course, the position of the psychoanalysis described here, and it is consequently inevitable that if this psychoanalysis ventures out into the world, it will be attacked. To take such a position will make no friends amongst those of a behavioural disposition when it comes to human affairs. Public policy makers are not likely to be impressed with the psychoanalyst's interest in his patient's state of mind, and analyses that continue for ten years or more.

Psychoanalysis is particularly likely to come into conflict with the institutions of psychological medicine and psychiatry. The psychiatric practitioner is searching for answers in the service of symptom relief, while the psychoanalytic practitioner is seeking understanding. Psychiatric practice is in the nature of an applied science; essentially goal directed, and utilitarian. Psychoanalytic practice, at least as it is being conceptualized here, is closer to that of a pure science; the analyst looks in the raw data of the session for meaning. Inherent in this search for meaning is the implication that there is something more to be understood, and such a perspective is subversive to the belief that one already possesses the knowledge and the answers to practical problems.

However, even when we look from the more 'utilitarian' perspective of change or outcome, nothing is straightforward. Many people would wish to believe that education, suggestion, encouragement, exhortation, coercion, and bullying should suffice to change people's so-called 'undesirable' behaviours or states of mind. In recent times we might add psychotropic drugs to this list. Nevertheless, it appears to be a fundamental truth of the human mind that none of this can substitute for understanding. The person who is in the habit of acting without thinking is not fulfilling their potential as a human being, and nothing can be substituted for the capacity to think. It is a fact that a baby cannot make use of education, exhortation and coercion; the baby can only make use of the mother's, or parent's, thoughtful attention, and the parent's understanding. The individual who, for whatever reason, has not had a sufficient experience of such attention as an infant, is rendered incapable of 'learning from experience', to take another phrase from Wilfred Bion (1962).

The dominant view in biological psychiatry relegates mind to an epiphenomenal position; that is, a kind of side-effect of the brain. Such a paradigm is essentially inimical to thinking. The relationship between mind and brain is conceptualized within the framework of a brain which 'causes' a mind, and the mind is then effected by means of interventions aimed at the brain. It is true that there are other paradigms within psychiatry, but it is also true that in practice, psychiatric interventions are very often based upon this assumption, explicit or implicit. Within this dominant paradigm, the mind is not considered as a source of mental disturbance or as an object worthy of investigation in its own right. Depression is a 'chemical thing', so what would be the point of thinking about what else it might mean? The Melbourne philosopher Tamas Pataki in an insightful and incisive paper entitled 'Psychoanalysis, Psychiatry, Philosophy', has commented:

> The ancient injunction which governs psychoanalysis is 'Know thyself'; but modern, biological psychiatry says: don't bother. (1996 p. 62)

Concluding thought

Psychic change is much more difficult than most of us imagine, perhaps more difficult than we can imagine. One reason is that psychic truth is often so difficult or painful to face. This remains true for the analyst as for the patient. Our self-importance is always a way of protecting ourselves from a more bitter reality. Before King Lear can face anything of this reality, he must first lose his kingly status and second risk losing his mind.

References

Bion, W. (1994). *Learning From Experience.* New Jersey: Jason Aronson. (Original work published 1962).

——— (1984). *Second Thoughts.* London: Karnac. (Original work published 1967).

——— (1984). *Attention and Interpretation.* London: Karnac. (Original work published 1970).

——— (1974). *Bion's Brazilian Lectures* (Vol. 1). Rio de Janeiro: Imago Editora.

Bloom, H. (1998). *Shakespeare: The Invention of the Human.* New York: Riverhead Books.

Collingwood, R.G. (1940). *An Essay on Metaphysics.* London: Oxford University Press.

Fairbairn, W.R.D. (1990). *Psychoanalytic Studies of the Personality.* London: Routledge. (Original work published 1943).

Freud, S. (1923a [1922]). Two encyclopaedia articles. In J. Strachey (Ed. & Trans.). *The Standard Edition of the Complete Psychological Works of Sigmund Freud* (Vol. 18). London: Hogarth Press.

——— (1912e [1912]). Recommendations to physicians practicing psycho-analysis. In J. Strachey (Ed. & Trans.). *The Standard Edition of the Complete Psychological Works of Sigmund Freud* (Vol. 12). London: Hogarth Press.

——— & Breuer, J. (1895d [1893–1895]). Studies on hysteria. In J. Strachey (Ed. & Trans.). *The Standard Edition of the Complete Psychological Works of Sigmund Freud* (Vol. 2). London: Hogarth Press.

Kant, I. (1977). J. W. Ellington (Ed.) *Prolegomena to any future metaphysics.* Indianapolis: Hackett Publishing. (Original work published 1783).

Motion, A. (1997). *Keats.* London: Faber and Faber.

Pataki, T. (1996). Psychoanalysis, psychiatry, philosophy. *Quadrant* 40(4):52–63.

Shakespeare, W. (1990). *Hamlet.* In S. Wells & G. Taylor (Eds.). *The Complete Oxford Shakespeare.* London: Oxford University Press. (Original work published c.1601).

——— (1990). *King Lear.* In S. Wells & G. Taylor (Eds.). In *The Complete Oxford Shakespeare.* London: Oxford University Press. (Original work published c.1606).

Symington, N. (2007). *Becoming a Person Through Psychoanalysis.* London: Karnac.

Winnicott, D.W. (1990). *The Maturational Processes and the Facilitating Environment.* London: Karnac. (Original work published 1960).

——— (1991). *Playing and Reality.* London: Routledge. (Original work published 1971).

'It Is Myself that I Remake': W.B. Yeats' Self Construction in Life and Poetry.

First published in: *British Journal of Psychotherapy*, vol 17, number 1, p 71-84: 2000

Abstract

W.B. Yeats is one of the pre-eminent poets in English of the twentieth century. His verse is characterised by its accessibility and emotional power, and a meticulous craftsmanship in the service of achieving the desired effect. Yeats paid a similarly workmanlike attention to the task of creating his own identity, in a self-conscious attempt to 'remake' himself. This paper examines Yeats' life and poetry in order to explore the psychological origins of both his artistic creativity and his need to remake himself. It looks beyond his identification with his father's literary and artistic ideals, to evidence from the poetry for an early developmental experience of absence or failure of the maternal function. The available biographical detail from Yeats' childhood and family is consistent with this conjecture.

In April 1934, at the age of sixty-eight, William Butler Yeats underwent a new surgical procedure, the Steinach operation. Suffering from impotence, probably depressed, and for some years unable to write any new poetry (Ellmann 1982, p.28), Yeats is said to have stated to a friend that he had no wish to go on living unless he could re-create himself continually, continually compete with himself (Hone 1942, p.436). The friend mentioned the new operation said to result in a physiological rejuvenation.

The Steinach procedure was no more than a modern-day vasectomy, but at the time was widely believed to have genuine physiological effects. After the operation Yeats, wishing to make up for what he termed the wasted nights of his youth (Jeffares 1990, p.266), embarked on several late life 'affairs', and dubbed this period his 'second puberty' (Ellmann 1982). His wife, Georgie Yeats, was aware of, and apparently prepared to tolerate, these liaisons. The little available evidence does not support Yeats' assertion of a significant beneficial effect on his impotence (Ellmann 1982, p.28; Lock 1983, p.1968); the Steinach operation presumably had no physiological effects in itself, acting rather as a placebo or 'magic' cure. The psychological effects, and benefits in engendering Yeats' creative energies, were however considerable, and he began writing poetry and plays with renewed vigour. The masterful poems written in the remaining five years of Yeats' life include many of his greatest, exploring his long-standing preoccupation with the dichotomies of life and death, body and soul, meaning and meaninglessness, and developing themes of corporeality and sexuality with new explicitness.

In his magnificent elegy *In Memory of W.B. Yeats*, W. H. Auden wrote, 'You were silly like us; your gift survived it all'. The episode of the Steinach operation and the second puberty attests to Yeats' 'silliness', but it equally manifests a self-understanding and, perhaps unconscious, wisdom; Yeats recognised what kind of treatment would be needed to 'remake' himself, and lift him out of his paralysis. The episode continued his life-long pattern of reliance on external sources of magic and power, and continued a life-long quest in search of the ideal love experience. It reflects the link, identified by Richard Ellmann (1982, p.28), between 'versemaking' and 'lovemaking' in Yeats' mind. Versemaking depended upon access to an intrapsychic source of creative energy that was linked with an ideal of a potent relationship with the feminine. In striving to banish the impotence of age, Yeats was also striving to banish the impotence of youth. Without the sense of vital renewal and the remaking of himself experienced through lovemaking and versemaking, he became vulnerable to depression.

This paper examines Yeats' life and poetry in an attempt to explore the psychological origins of his prodigious creativity. The gift of poetry and Yeats' 'silliness' are understood as differing but linked expressions of his deeply divided self. Yeats himself was very much aware of the unconscious origin of his own poetic impulse. In a letter to Dorothy Wellesley he wrote: 'We have all something within ourselves to batter down and get our power from this fighting.' This power, he continues, is a passion that depends upon the 'beast underneath', and the 'conflict is deep in my subconscious, perhaps in everybody's.' (Ellmann 1979, p.138)

A Search for the Maternal

> Nine bean-rows will I have there, a hive for the honey-bee,
> And live alone in the bee-loud glade.
> (*The Lake Isle of Innisfree*-1888)

Yeats was born in Dublin on 13th June 1865. In writing of Yeats' childhood, biographers have focused on the powerful figure of his father, John Butler Yeats. The father would seem to have been especially attached to his first born child: 'I think your birth was the first *great* event in my life,' he wrote to his son at the time of the birth of Yeats' first child: 'I never felt like that afterwards at the birth of the others.' (Foster 1997, p.15) Although particularly interested in and concerned with William's well-being, this was frequently expressed from a distance as he was more often than not in London, absent from the family home in Sligo. From the first, the father's influence would be powerful but erratic. When Yeats was nine his father moved the family, much against his wife's wishes, to London, and taking note that his son could not read, set about teaching him, sometimes by physical coercion (Ellmann 1979, p.25). He read poetry to him and sought to impose many of his views, including the idea that the highest form of literature was dramatic poetry (Ellmann 1979, p.27). The result of the father's domination was lifelong tension and quarrelling, but Yeats wrote later that in his teenage years he had admired his father above all men (Ellmann 1979, p.274), and he adopted much of his father's thinking.

Because the father provided the determining influence shaping the son's conscious mind, biographers have tended to underestimate the importance of the mother[1]. One reason for this is that Susan Yeats is a relatively absent figure from Yeats' own autobiographical writings, *Reveries over Childhood and Youth* (in *Autobiographies,* 1955). Within a psychoanalytic frame a sketchy or missing figure may be of the greatest importance, and there is evidence that Susan Yeats struggled to fulfil her maternal role. She was one of a family of twelve children who, at least according to John Butler Yeats, sat together, 'all disliking each other, at any rate alien mutually, in gloomy silence' (Murphy 1978, p.37). She has been described by her eldest daughter as 'not at all good at housekeeping and child-minding,' and further: 'She was prim and austere, suffered all in silence. She asked no sympathy and gave none....She endured and made no moan.' (Murphy 1978, p.215) Yeats' own childhood memory was that his mother would have considered any display of emotion 'a vulgarity' (1955, p.31). John Butler Yeats once wrote to his son that his wife's affection 'was a matter that one *inferred.* No one ever saw it or heard it speak' (Murphy 1978, p.215), and on another occasion to John Quinn:

> I used to tell her that if I had been lost for years and then suddenly presented myself she would have merely asked "Have you had your dinner?" All this is very like Willie. (Jeffares 1990, p.208)

Susan Yeats appears to have been emotionally undemonstrative, possessing a somewhat passive aggressive personality style. She was also prone to depression which she appears to have experienced increasingly through the course of her life. It seems likely she would not have naturally and easily provided the maternal functions of 'mirroring' and 'affective attunement' that are understood to be so essential to the integrity of the child's developing self (Stern 1985, p.138), nor was she likely to have received any help from her often absent husband. Yeats had a nurse as an infant although the major biographers give no indication of her importance. The intensity and completeness of Yeats' identification with his father in later childhood may in part reflect his inchoate sense of self at the time he came fully under his father's sway.

As a boy Yeats had a delicate constitution and suffered poor eyesight. In *Reveries over Childhood and Youth* he wrote that he remembered 'little of childhood but its pain', and that he had 'grown happier with every year of life as though gradually conquering something in myself,...' (1955, p.11). As a young child he sought solace in the countryside of Sligo, and the one positive attribute belonging to his mother as portrayed in his *Reveries* was her love for that countryside and its folk traditions.

'She would spend hours listening to stories or telling stories of the pilots and fishing-people of Rosses Point, or of her own Sligo girlhood, and it was always assumed between her and us that Sligo was more beautiful than other places.' (1955, p.31)

Yeats' own love affair with the Sligo countryside and Irish folklore was a direct and life-giving connection with his mother.

John Butler Yeats may have had his son in mind as much as himself, when he wrote in his unpublished memoirs:

> If it is deeply enquired into, I think it will be recognised that the foundation of the artistic nature is affectionateness which, denied

> its satisfaction, as it always is, in real life, turns to the invention of art and poetry. (Foster 1997, p.27)

In Yeats' much anthologised early poem *The Lake Isle of Innisfree* (1888), Innisfree is a place where mother nature provides for all needs and the poet can 'live alone in the bee-loud glade' free from complicating human relationship. There is imagined regression to a state of infantile dependence upon an idealised nurturing maternal function; where 'lake water lapping with low sounds by the shore' is a lullaby for the 'deep heart's core'. The poem suggests the dependency need of the poet, which it is feared cannot be satisfied by any human relationship.

One woman who touched the 'deep heart's core' was Lady Augusta Gregory, who took him under her wing when he visited Coole, her country estate, after breaking off his first consummated love affair, with Olivia Shakespeare. That Lady Gregory became a substitute maternal figure has been recognised by Norman Jeffares, who has written: 'Yeats had lacked mothering in his youth, and he now got that, in middle age, at Coole.' (1990, p.91) Lady Gregory was an assertive and independent widow. Alongside her maternal aspect she possessed those qualities Yeats found indispensable in his feminine ideal, and like the poet's mother, she possessed a passionate interest in the folk traditions of old Ireland.

In 1909 Lady Gregory became ill and nearly died. Yeats received a letter from her son Robert, whose writing he did not recognise at first. In his *Autobiographies* he recalls,

> I thought my mother was ill and that my sister was asking me to come at once: then I remembered that my mother died years ago and that more than kin was at stake. She [Lady Gregory] has been to me mother, friend, sister and brother. I cannot realise the world without her (1955, p.477).

It would seem Susan Yeats had never been a fully realised presence in her son's life, at least his conscious life, and thus he was unable to fully realise her death. Yeats recalled that her 'last fading out' after long illness made no noticeable change in his life (Jeffares 1990, p.133). In contrast it was Lady Gregory's death in 1932 that seemed to usher in the uncreative period (Jeffares 1990, p.256; Lock 1983, p.1965) that eventually led Yeats to pursue the Steinach operation.

Poetry and Love

> You think it horrible that lust and rage
> Should dance attendance upon my old age;
> They were not such a plague when I was young;
> What else have I to spur me into song?
> (*The Spur*-1936)

Whether as a somewhat effete young bard or as Ireland's eccentric elder poet-statesman, Yeats is often thought of as a poet preoccupied with the possibility of ideal love between a man and a woman. The dreamy romantic verses of his early 'Celtic Twilight' period express the fantasy of what was experienced as unattainable in reality. They are suffused with longing, while 'lust and rage' remain in the background. His first major poem, *The Wanderings of Oisin* (1887), is a lengthy romantic epic which reworks Irish folk-lore. In Jeffares' assessment it 'shows the poet in love with the idea of love, ready for a goddess to carry him off.' (Jeffares 1990, p.29) The goddess was personified in 1889 when Yeats, aged twenty-three, met Maud Gonne. She was a striking presence: tall, dark, beautiful, dogmatic and unconventional in thought, she shared Yeats' interest in the spirit realm, and was a prominent public figure in the cause of Irish nationalism. She served as a suitable figure for the poet's idealising projections, and Yeats immediately fell in love.

Gonne however was given to extremes. She believed violence an acceptable means to her political ends, and Jeffares has described her as ruthless and revolutionary (1990, p.40). From the beginning she would reject Yeats as a lover, while maintaining their often intimate friendship. In 1891 she wrote to him that she had dreamt of their being sister and brother in a past life (Foster 1997, p.114), and again in 1895 of their travelling to each other astrally (Foster 1997, p.157). What she did not tell Yeats in 1889 was that she was already involved in a relationship with a Frenchman, Lucien Millevoye, by whom she would have two children. Not until after the liaison with Millevoye had ended, in 1898, did she finally tell Yeats about it, at the same time insisting that she wished their relationship to remain a platonic one. She is purported to have given her aversion to sexual love as a reason (Foster 1997, p.203).

Whether or not the aversion was Maud's, it certainly belonged to Yeats; there was safety in being in love at a distance. Ellmann writes that in relation to Maud he 'thought of himself as full of weakness, and felt that if she loved him, unaware of his weaknesses, she would be deceived. The only solution was to love her in vain.' (1979, p.80). Foster also suggests that the ambivalence was not one-sided; that Yeats was more hesitant and uncertain than he could readily acknowledge (1997, p.203). He did however propose to Maud in 1891, and again on subsequent occasions, but was each time refused. Yeats came to think that he failed with Maud because he was not, nor could he style himself as, the assertive man of action. She reflected the hard edge he felt was lacking within himself and from his verse.

Being unable to consummate his passion for Maud was a 'solution' that suited Yeats in many respects. As an unattainable ideal she became a powerful muse: 'A girl arose that had red mournful lips / And seemed the greatness of the world in tears' (*The Sorrow of Love* -1891). It was not until

1896, when Yeats was thirty, that he finally abandoned celibate devotion to Maud to embark upon an affair with Olivia Shakespeare who, involved in an unhappy marriage herself, appears to have been the prime mover. Yeats' ongoing preoccupation with Maud eventually led Olivia to break off the liaison, but she would remain a lifelong friend and confidante.

The beginning of a deeper psychological rupture was forced in 1903 when Maud, unexpectedly to Yeats, married Major John MacBride. Yeats possessed a low estimation of MacBride, and his idealisation of Maud was correspondingly diminished. He would eventually respond with a measure of rejection towards her; in unpublished lines (Jeffares 1990, p.109) she became the woman who 'taught me hate / By kisses to a clown'. This conscious awareness of anger, and a lessened idealisation, allowed Yeats to retrieve some of the potency that had been projectively identified in her. He took up the sexual relationship with Olivia Shakespeare again, and other affairs were to follow. Ellmann has identified the consequent change in the verse of the plays he was writing, 'which for the first time introduces a sexual theme without occult or Pre-Raphaelite camouflage.' (Ellmann 1979, p.179)

Although weakened, Maud's hold over Yeats remained. Her marriage proved disastrous, and she eventually separated from MacBride in 1905. Maud and Yeats almost certainly did have a brief sexual liaison late in 1908, (Ellmann 1979, p.xxvi; Foster 1997, p.393) but, at least for Maud, no permanent union was possible.

By 1908, at the time of writing *No Second Troy*, there was sufficient distance for a less idealised picture of Maud, and Yeats had begun to find a more assertive voice. It is perhaps the best known of the series of poems in which Maud is personified as Helen, whose great beauty gave rise to the Trojan wars. Yeats emphasises her martial aspects, but his idealisation is tempered by ambivalence about the destructive capacities portrayed, and his blame towards her is implicit.

No Second Troy

Why should I blame her that she filled my days
With misery, or that she would of late
Have taught to ignorant men most violent ways,
Or hurled the little streets upon the great,
Had they but courage equal to desire?
What could have made her peaceful with a mind
That nobleness made simple as a fire,
With beauty like a tightened bow, a kind
That is not natural in an age like this,
Being high and solitary and most stern?
Why, what could she have done, being what she is?
Was there another Troy for her to burn?

F.A.C. Wilson has commented that throughout Yeats' courtship with Maud, he responded erotically to her hard and masculine side, adopting himself 'a passive and studiously feminine stance towards it.' (1972, p.6) Wilson has identified that Yeats' poetic representations of Maud, and of his feminine ideal, are consistently impregnated with this masculine or 'martial' element, and has formulated this in terms of Yeats' need to find as the object of his love someone who combined the characteristics of both sexes. Wilson has observed that after Maud's marriage to MacBride the pattern of submission before the feminine in Yeats' poems gives way to a 'semi-sadistic' one, with the 'sense of fruitful antagonism between lover and beloved, often expressing itself through animal rape-imagery' (1972, p.6). *Leda and the Swan* (1923), portraying the mythical rape of Leda by the God Zeus in the guise of a swan, is the culmination of this development. Rape binds lust and rage, and the development of such themes reinforces the impression that Yeats' increasing sexual freedom from the time of Maud's marriage was associated with some weakening of the domination of an unconscious 'aggressive' feminine imago, and increased conscious access to his own aggressive energies.

In the aftermath of the abortive 1916 Irish uprising, John MacBride, as one of the ringleaders, was executed by firing squad. In his poem *Easter 1916* Yeats recorded his response to these events; MacBride, along with the other rebels, is praised for his valour, but characterised, with good reason (Foster 1997, p.330), as 'A drunken, vainglorious lout.' These events opened the way for a final proposal to Maud, but again he was refused. At fifty-two, Yeats was feeling under pressure. He proposed to Maud's daughter, Iseult Gonne, born from the liaison with Millevoye, and with whom he enjoyed a close relationship. After some hesitation, Iseult refused. He sought council with Lady Gregory, then proposed to Georgie Hyde-Lees, a woman towards whom he had a genuine attraction, and who he believed would be satisfied with him. She accepted and they married in 1917; Georgie Hyde-Lees was twenty-five.

Yeats was in a state of great agitation during the first days of their honeymoon. Had he made the right choice in not waiting and pursuing the possibility of marriage to Iseult Gonne? Georgie, or George, as Yeats preferred to call his wife, possessed a fine intuition, and moreover she shared Yeats' interest in the occult. She responded to the crisis by 'discovering' in herself a gift for automatic writing that allowed her to receive messages from the 'spirit world'. Yeats described the events in a letter to Lady Gregory:

She said she felt that something was to be written through her. She got a piece of paper, and talking to me all the while so that her thoughts would not affect what she wrote, wrote these words (which she did not understand), "with the bird" (Iseult) "all is well at heart. Your action was right for both but in London you mistook its meaning." (Jeffares 1990, p.182)

Georgie Yeats' account of events differed in the content of the message, which Ellmann states she remembered years later as approximately: 'What you have done is right for both the cat and the hare.' (Ellmann 1979, p.xvi)

According to Georgie Yeats, once she had written the initial message the writing continued irresistibly (Ellmann 1979, p.xvi), and what began as deliberate deception on her part became truly 'automatic'. Yeats believed the message miraculous and experienced great psychological relief, as well as equally miraculous relief from troublesome fatigue, rheumatic pains and neuralgia (Jeffares 1990, p.182). He subsequently persuaded his wife to spend up to several hours a day over a period of years in this state of suspended consciousness receiving the 'messages', and although the material was often obscure, once reworked by Yeats it became the foundation for his eccentric treatise on spirituality and metaphysics entitled *A Vision*.

Despite the shaky start, the marriage was apparently successful, at least in the early years; two children were born, and Yeats began to draw from a deeper well of poetic inspiration and imagery, writing ever more searching and accomplished poetry. The death of Lady Gregory in 1932 seems to have marked the beginning of the unproductive period that culminated with the Steinach operation; following this loss, and in the face of anxieties about loss of potency, failing health, and his own death, Yeats was to return to the elusive pursuit of a feminine ideal in the 'affairs' of his 'second puberty'.

Masterbuilder of the Self

The friends that have it I do wrong
Whenever I remake a song,
Should know what issue is at stake:
It is myself that I remake.
(Untitled verse)

Yeats' marriage to Georgie Hyde-Lees represented the final relinquishing of the possibility of marriage with either Maud or her surrogate Iseult.

Being unable to perceive in Georgie the qualities that conformed to his feminine ideal, he was beset by a crippling doubt, which the automatic writing served to dispel. For Yeats it symbolised his wife's capacity to access a source of power and authority that in turn energised and reassured him. It is possible to offer this interpretation with some confidence because out of these events Yeats wrote a poem, his long epithalamium entitled *The Gift of Harun Al-Rashid.*

In this allegorical poem the central figure, Kusta Ben Luka, takes a young bride in his old age. The bride is portrayed as an archetype of modest femininity, but soon she falls into strange night-time trances during which she articulates mysterious truths. Kusta attributes the origin of the trances to the influence of a male Djinn:

> Or was it she that spoke or some great Djinn?
> I say that a Djinn spoke. A livelong hour
> She seemed the learned man and I the child;

Richard Ellmann has speculated that the metapsychological function of the spirit world and magic for Yeats was as a source of legitimising masculine authority and strength compensating for the sense of vulnerability that was the legacy of his father's domination (1979, p.64). That the voice from the spirit world is a male one is consistent with Ellmann's hypothesis, however the focus of the poem invites another level of interpretation. Before and after the trances, the bride is portrayed as wholly feminine and naive, in 'childish ignorance' of her own transformations. The trances are more than possession by a masculine presence; they reveal a latent masculine and potentially aggressive element within the archetypal feminine ideal. The poem ends:

> And now my utmost mystery is out.
> A woman's beauty is a storm-tossed banner;

Under it wisdom stands, and I alone-
Of all Arabia's lovers I alone-
Nor dazzled by the embroidery, nor lost
in the confusion of its night-dark folds,
Can hear the armed man speak.

The singular importance of the 'utmost mystery' would seem to be that without this revelation of a masculine, martial element, the archetypal feminine ideal cannot fully engage the Kusta-Yeats figure of the poem. Even the 'night-dark folds' of the bride's sexuality seem to be ambivalently regarded, and are portrayed as inimical to the revelation of the 'utmost mystery'.

For Yeats the transformation of experience into poetry altered the nature of that experience; it was part of his construction of the myth of himself, and of the creation of what he referred to as the 'mask' (Ellmann 1979, p.172); a process exemplified in the transformation of the events of his marriage and Georgie's 'discovery' of the automatic writing into *The Gift of Harun Al-Rashid.* Just as uncertainty and doubt were dispelled by the automatic writing, so they are absent from the poem, and from the myth of the poet. In *A General Introduction to my Work* (in *Essays and Introductions*) Yeats wrote that the poet is 'never the bundle of accident and incoherence that sits down to breakfast; he has been reborn as an idea, something intended, complete' (Yeats 1961, p.509). Poetry served to make the parts cohere.

Yeats claimed that when he was twenty-four the sentence: 'Hammer your thoughts into unity' formed in his mind: 'For days I could think of nothing else, and for years I tested all I did by that sentence.' (Ellmann 1979, p.237) As a young man Yeats experienced his outward self as lacking in potency, as if inhibited and enfeebled by his inward self of contemplation and hesitation (Ellmann 1979, p.75; Foster 1997, p.427). His solution was to strive consciously to remake himself, creating 'Unity of Being' within the outward self, which he would later designate the 'mask'. 'Unity of Being' was in fact an ideal originally espoused by John Butler Yeats (Ellmann 1979, p.236).

The remaking Yeats refers to in the untitled verse quoted was the constant rewriting of poems and verse plays with which he had become dissatisfied. These songs, being part of the mask, were part of himself, to be hammered into conformity with his changing conscious attitudes and conceptions. Yeats was indefatigable in his quest for the right word in the right place: 'A line will take us hours maybe; / Yet if it does not seem a moment's thought, / Our stitching and unstitching has been naught' (*Adam's Curse* 1902). More than the song was at stake.

In his *Autobiographies* Yeats wrote:

> I think all happiness depends on the energy to assume the mask of some other self; that all joyous or creative life is a rebirth as something not oneself, something which has no memory and is created in a moment and perpetually renewed. (1955, p.503)

For Yeats the creative life of poetry was a means of perpetual renewal, and this renewal as something 'not oneself', from somewhere that has 'no memory', suggests the source of poetic inspiration in the timeless unconscious. Access to this source was essential:

I think all happiness and 'all joyous or creative life' Yeats insists depend upon it, but it is also an energy employed to 'assume the mask of some other self'; a 'rebirth as something not oneself'. That this 'other self' can be revealed only as a 'mask', that it is in some essence 'not oneself', suggests something less than achievement of 'Unity of Being'. It also suggests Yeats' ambivalence towards this unconscious wellspring of creative energy. His concept of the 'mask' designated the outward self and action, but it also contained the idea of the consciously adopted role, and as such suggests something of Winnicott's 'false self' (1960).

For Yeats the mask, and the poems as part of the mask, would seem to have constituted a kind of compromise. It reflected and expressed another self, but as a creation, or even disguise, under the conscious control of its author, it was maintained at a necessary distance from that other self. Poetic inspiration, by providing access to an unconscious source, energised the mask and the outward life, but at the same time the source of energy was felt to be dangerous and in need of tight control.

A Divided Self

Turning and turning in the widening gyre
The falcon cannot hear the falconer;
Things fall apart; the centre cannot hold;
Mere anarchy is loosed upon the world,
The blood-dimmed tide is loosed, and everywhere
The ceremony of innocence is drowned;
The best lack all conviction, while the worst
Are full of passionate intensity.

Surely some revelation is at hand;
Surely the Second Coming is at hand.
The Second Coming! Hardly are those words out
When a vast image out of *Spiritus Mundi*
Troubles my sight: somewhere in sands of the desert
A shape with lion body and the head of a man,
A gaze blank and pitiless as the sun,
Is moving its slow thighs, while all about it

Reel shadows of the indignant desert birds.
The darkness drops again; but now I know
That twenty centuries of stony sleep
Were vexed to nightmare by a rocking cradle,
And what rough beast, its hour come round at last,
Slouches toward Bethlehem to be born?

The Second Coming is the one poem in Yeats' oeuvre which seems to address itself to the question of the nature of the subterranean and threatening force in the psyche; the 'beast underneath', that Yeats refers to in his letter to Dorothy Wellesley.

Harold Bloom has identified 'something in the power of *The Second Coming* that persuades us of our powerlessness.' (1970, p.324) Like many commentators he explores the origin of the poem in a socio-historical context, but comments 'what I hear in the poem is exultation on the speaker's part as he beholds his vision, and this exaltation is not only an intellectual one.' (1970, p.321) A psychoanalytic approach is required in order to conceptualise the nature of the poem's peculiar inherent power, which Richard Wheeler has argued arises out of its ability to access, 'a deeply repressed fantasy of omnipotent, destructive rage, called into service to master an experience of intolerable, infantile helplessness.'(1974, p.234)

The 'revelation' of the second stanza, after which 'the darkness drops again', has the quality of a dream. The vision itself invites symbolic interpretation, and is presented as of potential universal relevance in its origin from *Spiritus Mundi*, the collective storehouse of images which represented for Yeats something akin to Jung's collective unconscious. The conflict is 'deep in my subconscious, perhaps in everybody's', Yeats wrote to Wellesley.

As Wheeler suggests, the 'ceremony of innocence' is surely the benign state of experienced satisfaction and fusion between mother and infant.

This is the deepest need expressed in the poem, but it is a 'centre' that 'cannot hold'. The measured loss of control of the first four lines serves as a representation of, and invitation to, regression to the point where 'anarchy is loosed' and the benign state of symbiosis is split, the good elements becoming impotent, and the 'worst' full of destructive energy. The split suggests the 'paranoid-schizoid' position of infancy (Klein 1952), with a feared outcome of annihilation. Wheeler speculates that the terror originates in the oral-sadistic stage when 'good and bad potentialities...are created out of the dissolving symbiosis of infant and mother.' (1974, p.236) The intensity of the aggression created by the withholding of the nurturing mother/breast, and the dissolving symbiosis, is a ' "blood dimmed tide" which threatens to overwhelm or swallow up the aggressor.' (1974, p.237)

Release comes as the ruthless and intolerable aggression of the first stanza is projected into the representation of the beast in the second with its gaze 'blank and pitiless as the sun'. As differentiation of self and object begins, the 'paranoid-schizoid' drama of stanza one is maintained in stanza two, and a 'depressive' synthesis is not achieved. The object that comes into existence, the beast, like an Egyptian Sphinx, has the body of a lion and the head of a man. It has human features but is less than human. In Winnicott's language, a 'capacity for concern' (1963) has not emerged out of the state of infantile ruthlessness.

The hybrid Sphinx is also sexually suggestive. Wheeler comments that the image of the beast moving its slow thighs, 'concentrates and conveys the threatening power which the child associates with parental sexuality', and he offers an Oedipal dimension of interpretation of the Sphinx as a primal scene fantasy (1974, p.242). The Sphinx is a symbol of knowledge, and the knowledge of the 'rough beast' that is achieved in the revelation of stanza two is a knowledge of forces both malevolent and sexual. The hybrid nature of the sphinx seems suggestive of the blurring of identity that results when projective and introjective mechanisms prevent sufficient differentiation of self and object.

This interpretation of the poem, as depicting a process of entering into and emerging from a regressive fragmentation, suggests a latent potential within the poet. The loss of the self, and the rough beast that might be confronted in such a process, are ambivalently regarded. Such a potential is threatening, but the poem also suggests the possibility that regression into the 'paranoid-schizoid' organisation, and restitution of the beast within, are a means towards restoration of the self. The 'rough beast' is to be born at Bethlehem, the antithesis of the birth of Christ, and Christianity represents 'twenty centuries of stony sleep' in its inability to incorporate the beast, or shadow side, within the self. Yeats found common ground with Nietzsche in asserting the value of 'passionate intensity', even if destructive, against the impotence that results when 'the best lack all conviction'.

Wheeler (1974, p.250) has also pointed out the significant placement of the poem *A Prayer For My Daughter* (1919) immediately after *The Second Coming* in the volume *Michael Robartes and The Dancer*. In this poem Yeats contemplates the threat of a storm raging outside to his young daughter sleeping peacefully inside. She becomes a symbol of 'radical innocence', and as the poet wishes for her well-being he imagines her life's possible future directions and false turns, and reflects upon his own hard-won knowledge that 'to be choked with hate / May well be of all evil chances chief':

> Considering that, all hatred driven hence,
> The soul recovers radical innocence
> And learns at last that it is self-delighting,
> Self-appeasing, self-affrighting,
> And that its own sweet will is Heaven's will;
> She can, though every face should scowl

and every windy quarter howl
Or every bellows burst, be happy still.

The 'ceremony of innocence' that could not hold in *The Second Coming* is recovered, as 'radical innocence' in this companion poem through the driving out of the beast of hatred. Division and limitation within the poet's self are transcended through vicarious participation in his daughter's apparent innocence and unity.

The compulsive quality of Yeats' lifelong need to recreate himself; to achieve 'Unity of Being', suggests a divided self. Although the manner of its expression changed through time, the need to create unity out of division is both an insistent and consistent theme in Yeats' poetry. Many of the late poems work through a dialectical process of thesis and antithesis, based on the antinomy of active participation in life versus the withdrawal inherent in the spiritual and intellectual position, towards moments of synthesis, whereby division is transcended, often through acceptance of the limitations and suffering inherent in the human condition. At such moments of synthesis Yeats' poetry achieves great emotional intensity, distinct from the exaltation of power felt in *The Second Coming*. In the final stanza of *Among School Children* (1926):

Labour is blossoming or dancing where
The body is not bruised to pleasure soul,

and in the final line synthesis is for a moment complete, precluding division:

How can we know the dancer from the dance?

A persisting inner 'paranoid-schizoid' split offers a possible psychological formulation of the ultimate source of division and ambivalence that pervades things Yeatsian: outward physical objective reality juxtaposed to inward psychical subjective reality; body juxtaposed to spirit or soul; the participation of the active life against the withdrawal of the contemplative life; idealism versus realism. All these antinomies may be understood, in part, as reflecting the opposition between an aggressive participation in life and fearful withdrawal towards schizoid isolation. The moments of epiphany in Yeats' poetry are those when such dichotomies are transcended and a 'depressive' synthesis achieved, but in a psychological sense the unity thus created was a centre that could not hold; it had to be remade again and again.

Where all the ladders start

> When a man grows old his joy
> Grows more deep day after day,
> His empty heart is full at length,
> But he has need of all that strength
> Because of the increasing Night
> That opens her mystery and fright.
> (*The Apparitions*)

The Second Coming has been read as a representation of the ruthless rage and persecutory anxiety belonging to the unintegrated or 'paranoid-schizoid' state, that occurs when the capacities of the self are overwhelmed by experiences of frustration and trauma. To the extent that such experience cannot be satisfactorily encompassed by, and integrated into, the developing self, it remains split off from consciousness as a latent vulnerability or potential. In his *Journal* (published in *Memoirs*) Yeats comments on his own powerful aggressive impulses and their inhibition:

> The feeling is always the same: a consciousness of energy, of certainty, and of transforming power stopped by a wall, by something one must either submit to or rage against helplessly. It often alarms me; is it the root of madness? (Yeats 1972, p.157)

To a greater or lesser extent the persecutory anxieties of the 'paranoid-schizoid position' are a universally latent human experience, and this resonance in the collective unconscious, the origin out of '*Spiritus Mundi*', has been suggested as a reason for *The Second Coming*'s particular power and fascination for readers. In relation to Yeats himself the poem suggests that the 'beast underneath' has its origins in his own early experience.

The 'beast' was a source of energy and fascination, but also something to be 'battered down', with a resulting experience of depletion of the conscious self. In order to become successfully engaged in a love relationship Yeats needed to be able to recognise, and draw upon, a compensatory source of potency within the feminine. A consequent pattern of idealisation in his relationships with women can be discerned in the poetry as in life. At the same time it was only by risking involvement in a love relationship that a possibility for the restitution of this projected potency was created. Thus the breakdown of Yeats' idealisation in relation to Maud was accompanied by greater access to his capacity to 'hate', and a consequent increase in psychic freedom and creative potency.

A second freeing up of his creative energies followed his marriage. As well as being able to 'magically' conform to Yeats' feminine ideal, Georgie Yeats provided a maternal and holding function which served to stabilise Yeats' narcissistically vulnerable self, in a way that would have been impossible with Maud. The episode of the automatic writing reflects both Yeats' ongoing need to draw upon a source of power outside of himself, and Georgie's intuitive capacity for understanding that need. R.F. Foster has titled the first of his two volume Yeats biography *The Apprentice Mage*, and magic was one of Yeats' enduring preoccupations; he was involved with spiritualism and magic societies throughout his adult life, particularly the Hermetic Order of the Golden Dawn. Magic and spiritualism provided a further source of idealised power to draw on, when he experienced himself as vulnerable or threatened by depression. Perhaps without the psychological boost of the Steinach operation we might have been denied the magnificent poems of Yeats' 'second puberty'. In this regard Stephen Lock has wryly suggested, 'we should perhaps be thankful that Yeats escaped modern medicine.' (Lock 1983, p.1967)

The writing of poetry might be conceptualised as providing dual, and paradoxically opposed, functions for Yeats. As a means of access to unconscious potentials and energies, it facilitated growth and development within his self; while as part of the construction of an identity or 'mask' it provided a defensive or idealising function which, through the achievement of unity in art, protected against breakdown or fragmentation of the self. In the journal entry commenting on his inhibition of his own aggressive impulses, Yeats goes on to link his development of style to the transformation of this energy:

> There was a time when they [his writings] were threatened by it; I had to subdue a kind of Jacobin rage. I escaped from it all as a writer through my sense of style. Is not one's art made out of the struggle in one's soul? Is not beauty a victory over oneself? (Yeats 1972, p.157)

Yeats' need for the transforming magic of poetry remained undiminished throughout his life. Not only lust and rage, but death too, became a potent spur, and as he looked towards the end, he wrote. He had always hoped for evidence from his occult studies for the survival of the soul after death, but for Yeats as poet, the pursuit of the question and of a vision was more important than any certain answer: 'and yet when all is said /

It was the dream itself enchanted me', he reflects in *The Circus Animals' Desertion* (1938). But the anticipation of death was also a powerful foil to enchantment, and it is concrete and corporeal reality that comes to have the increasingly powerful claim. In *A Dialogue of Self and Soul* (1927), the Self has the final and more convincing voice:

> I am content to live it all again
> And yet again, if it be life to pitch
> Into the frog-spawn of a blind man's ditch,
> A blind man battering blind men;

In *The Circus Animals' Desertion* Yeats ostensibly laments the loss of his 'ladder' which gave access to fantasies and images of enchantment, his 'circus animals', but the power of the poem's final and heroic couplet is born from the recognition that true creativity lies in the embrace of what cannot be avoided:

> Now that my ladder's gone
> I must lie down where all the ladders start
> In the foul rag and bone shop of the heart.

Yeats' compulsive need to remake himself, and by implication his sense of himself as incomplete, has been identified. At the deepest level, this lifetime striving for 'Unity of Being' might be understood as an expression of the need to heal the violence of a 'paranoid-schizoid' division within the self, and to reaffirm the possibility, at least intrapsychically, of an non-conflicted union with the maternal. The interpretation of Yeats' poetry as reflecting an intrapsychic experience of maternal failure or loss must stand on the poetry alone. Nevertheless it seems significant that available biographical information about Yeats' childhood and family, suggests an atmosphere of emotional attenuation, where maternal preoccupation was at a premium, and linked to Susan Yeats' passion for the folk traditions of old Ireland.

At the end of *Reveries over Childhood and Youth*, Yeats expressed poignantly his sense of an unfinished life, and linked this sentiment with his childhood experience. He wrote that thinking about his childhood had left him 'sorrowful and disturbed', and his final sentence concludes: 'all life weighed in the scales of my own life seems to me a preparation for something that never happens.' (1955, p.106) Could it be that the need to remake himself, by transcending division and incompleteness within, was a necessary source of Yeats' artistic creativity, and that without it we would not have received the gift of his poetry?

Notes

Subsequent to writing this paper I have read Brenda Maddox's recent (1999) biography, *George's Ghosts: A New Life of W.B. Yeats* (London: Picador).

Maddox also identifies the tendency of biographers to overlook the importance of the mother, and gives detailed consideration to the biographical evidence as to Susan Yeats' influence upon her son's life. It is of note that her analysis leads to similar formulations to those put forward in this paper.

References

Bloom, H. (1970) *Yeats.* New York: Oxford University Press.

Ellmann, R. (1979) *Yeats: The Man and the Masks.* Oxford: Oxford University Press.

—Ellmann, R. (1982) W.B. Yeats's Second Puberty. In *Four Dubliners.* London: Hamish Hamilton.

Foster, R. F. (1997) *W.B. Yeats: A Life-Vol 1: The Apprentice Mage.* Oxford: Oxford University Press.

Hone, J. (1942) *W.B. Yeats 1865-1939.* London: Macmillan.

Jeffares, A.N. (1990) *W.B. Yeats: A New Biography.* London: Arena.

Klein, M. (1952) Some Theoretical Conclusions Regarding the Emotional Life of the Infant. reprinted in *Envy and Gratitude and Other Works: 1946-1963.* (1975) London: Hogarth Press.

Lock, S. (1983) "O that I were young again": Yeats and the Steinach operation. *British Medical Journal* 287: 1964-8.

Murphy, W.M. (1978) *Prodigal Father: The Life of John Butler Yeats (1839-1922).* Ithaca and London: Cornell University Press.

Stern, D. (1985) *The Interpersonal World of the Infant.* New York: Basic Books.

Wheeler, R.P. (1974) Yeats' "Second Coming": What Rough Beast? In *American Imago* 31(3): 233-251.

Wilson, F.A.C. (1972) Yeats's "A Bronze Head": A Freudian Investigation. In *Literature and Psychology* 22(1): 5-12.

Winnicott, D. W. (1960) Ego Distortion in Terms of True and False Self. Reprinted in *The Maturational Processes and the Facilitating Environment.* (1990) London: Karnac.

—Winnicott, D. W. (1963) The Development of the Capacity for Concern. Reprinted in: *The Maturational Processes and the Facilitating Environment.* (1990) London: Karnac.

Yeats, W. B. (1955) *Autobiographies.* London: Macmillan.

—Yeats, W. B. (1961) *Essays and Introductions.* London: Macmillan.

—Yeats, W. B. (1972) (Ed: Denis Donoghue) *Memoirs* London: Macmillan.

Psychoanalysis and psychotherapy: a personal view

"... the beginning of health is the knowledge of the disease, and the patient's desire to comply with the physician's prescription. You are now in the diseased condition, sensible of your infirmity, and heaven, or rather God himself, who is the great physician, will apply those medicines which are proper to the cure of your distemper; but, these remedies are wont to operate slowly, not in a sudden and miraculous manner. And sensible sinners are much more likely to recover, than delinquents of little understanding. Now, as your discourse evinces your discretion, be of good cheer, and courageously wait for the perfect recovery of your conscience."

Cervantes—*Don Quixote*, 1605, reprinted 1986

These words, from the fertile and febrile mind of Cervantes' Don Quixote, suggest that, at the beginning of the 17th century, Cervantes was well aware of the relationship between psychoanalysis and cure.

We may note certain themes:

It is knowledge of the disease which is the beginning of health.

All are sinners but the real delinquency is the destruction of understanding.

Those who expect sudden and miraculous cures are subject to delusion and liable to disappointment.

Both patient and physician must relinquish omnipotence before a greater power.

Patience and courage seem to be required.

Neville Symington's paper, *The Difference Between Psychotherapy and Psychoanalysis* (2004) begins with an attempt to distinguish something called 'psychotherapy' and something called 'psychoanalysis'. Symington's suggested basis for the distinction is that psychotherapy is something pursued with the intention of helping a person to feel better while psychoanalysis is something pursued with the intention of furthering self-awareness. While Symington makes compelling points regarding the nature of psychoanalysis, his attempt to distinguish psychotherapy from psychoanalysis seems to me not to stand up to analysis. In particular his assertion that psychotherapy is cure by suggestion seems problematic. Symington defines a psychotherapeutic cure as reliant on suggestion with the intention of helping a person to feel better, however at the same time Symington seems to make it clear that 'feeling better' and achieving real cure within the psyche are not the same thing.

Techniques of suggestion are compatible neither with the analytic attitude that Symington describes nor the therapeutic attitude that Cervantes describes. As Cervantes suggests the 'physician's prescription' and the 'medicines proper' to cure are, unlike suggestion, 'wont to operate slowly' and 'not in a sudden miraculous manner'. It is, I think, misleading to link techniques that rely on suggestion with the term psychotherapy and the possibility of cure.

What is Psychoanalysis?

Symington raises this question specifically in the realm of the clinical encounter and treatment. I will adopt his terminology, and also that of Cervantes, and use the terms patient and physician, rather that analysand

and analyst. 'Patient' and 'physician' preserve a focus on the therapeutic dimension of clinical psychoanalysis.

Psychoanalysis, Symington suggests, can be defined by the presence of a process of working towards self-awareness. As he points out the process of arriving at such knowledge or understanding is clearly something different from an activity driven by a wish for the patient to feel better. This need not exclude the possibility of the patient being motivated in some sense by the wish to feel better, nor does it necessarily exclude the possibility of the physician being so motivated at a 'sublimated' level, nevertheless, in order for the work of analysis to progress the patient must eventually arrive at a point where analysis is privileged over what is comfortable. That is to say, a point where what is true is valued more than the avoidance of what is uncomfortable or painful. The physician, it is hoped, is identified with this position from the outset.

In practice the usual situation is probably that the patient moves towards and retreats from such a position from session to session and moment to moment. Thus, the point at which useful analytic work is taking place is not simply one that is arrived at once and for all. The process of analysis is an on-going struggle of ambivalence, moving towards and retreating from the analytic task. Assuming the physician is competent to the task, then the analytic work becomes in a sense embodied in the presence of the physician, and this to and fro relationship with the work becomes linked to a process of emotional engagement and disengagement with the physician.

Symington emphasizes the point that none of this is contingent upon such apparently characteristic features of the psychoanalytic set up such as the use of the couch, the fifty-minute session, or the frequency of sessions four or five times a week. As he suggests one physician might be able to achieve more with a particular patient in once a week sessions than another physician in five times a week sessions. The conclusion would seem to be that it is possible to choose to define clinical psychoanalysis by concrete criteria such as frequency of sessions, but such definitions would be poor ones. For the reasons Symington outlines, clinical psychoanalysis is perhaps best defined by the presence of what we might call 'psychoanalytic work'. Psychoanalytic work would be recognized as such by the movement towards, rather than away from, the truth; a movement towards self-awareness. While such psychoanalytic work might be favoured by frequent, rather than infrequent, sessions, it is nevertheless possible in a variety of different frames. A single session, even a single encounter, provides a potential space for the development of analytic work, and within which such work might take place. The frame is secondary to the person of the physician.

Psychoanalytic work is characterized by movement towards the truth. No sooner do we attempt a generalization such as this than all sorts of problems present themselves. What about the situation where the patient comes for help, perhaps even considering that they are coming for an 'analysis', while the physician considers that the patient's mind seems to be organized around 'untruth' and not knowing about themselves? Let us assume for the sake of the argument that the physician's judgment is accurate. In order for psychoanalytic work to develop in such a situation a great deal of preparatory work may be required, perhaps over many years; patience and tact may be required on the part of the physician. The early stages of the process may be, for example, characterized by a desperate dependence on the part of the patient, with little evidence of a wish to know more about anything. Can this preparatory work, when there is little evidence of a psychoanalytic capacity within the patient, be considered psychoanalysis? I would suggest that if this initial work is informed by the physician's analysis of what is likely to facilitate the development of a psychoanalytic process with this particular patient, and that this end is kept continually in mind, then this is psychoanalytic work and the process is psychoanalysis. I think that the place where we must look initially for the defining characteristics of a psychoanalytic process is the mind of the physician. It is the patient's task to get to a session, but the commitment and the capacity to facilitate a psychoanalytic process within the session is primarily the business of the physician.

With regard to the idea that the physician's task is to help the patient come to know himself, this might be reframed slightly: the physician's task is to facilitate a process within which it becomes possible for the patient to come to know himself.

What is psychotherapy?

If I ask myself this question, Symington's answer—that psychotherapy is defined by the intention of helping someone to feel better—is not one that would immediately occur to me. However, it seems possible that many people who regard themselves as practitioners of one form of psychotherapy or another might hold a view more or less along these lines. It may be that most such practitioners would take this view, but even if this were so can we regard the definition as valid simply on the basis that it is a popular, or even a majority view?

The word psychotherapy suggests its own definition and it would seem more fruitful to begin with the word itself. *The Shorter Oxford English Dictionary* offers the following definition: 'The treatment of disorders of emotion or personality by psychological methods'.

'Psycho' plus 'therapy' seems to suggest, either therapy provided by specifically psychological means, or therapy specifically directed to the psyche. Combining these ideas would suggest the word to mean psychologically-based therapy of the psyche. This leads us to consider what therapy might mean, or in other words, what is therapeutic. Again, the *Oxford Dictionary* suggests that something therapeutic is 'a curative agent; a healing influence'. So, what is healing or curative of the mind or psyche?

My view is that what is healing of the mind is the kind of knowledge and experience that leads to growth and/or integration, that is self-awareness.

It can be observed that certain persons seem to be able to derive a benefit from an experience of adversity. Someone who crashes a car through carelessness might be led to reflect upon his or her vulnerability and capacities, and become a more careful driver as a result. To the extent that such an experience leads someone to reflect upon his or her omnipotent assumptions it could be regarded as healing. When someone experiences a major loss and works through the consequent process of grief, he or she will be a different person subsequently. It is widely recognized that grief experiences can lead to a strengthening and deepening of the mind. Unsought experiences such as these, while they do not constitute an intentional form of therapy, nevertheless appear to have a 'therapeutic' potential for the mind. They seem to possess this potential even though we might characterize such experiences as leading someone to feel worse, rather than feel better. It is clear that there is no necessary link between what is 'therapeutic', and 'feeling better', and 'feeling better' cannot be considered as a defining characteristic of what is therapeutic, or 'psychotherapeutic'.

We similarly recognize that within the clinical encounter, what Cervantes refers to as the necessary 'knowledge of the disease' does not necessarily carry the direct effect of the patient feeling better. The patient may profess to feel very much worse as a result of the 'physician's prescription'.

Fairbairn (1943) has argued that analytic technique can be conceptualized as designed to facilitate 'a release of repressed bad objects from the unconscious', but 'it is also fear of just such a release that characteristically drives the patient to seek analytical aid in the first instance', so that if a successful therapeutic process ensues 'It is only when the released bad objects are beginning to lose their terror for him that he really begins to appreciate the virtue of mental immunization therapy.' By 'release' here Fairbairn is referring to release from the unconscious, hence making the unconscious

conscious. The potential therapeutic effect of either 'psychoanalysis' or 'psychotherapy' lies in the integration that ensues from the process. As recognized such integration is often resisted for a variety of reasons, not least being that it is uncomfortable and painful.

This, as I understand it, is essentially what Symington suggests when he says that awareness of our own madness is the goal of psychoanalysis. It is also such awareness which carries therapeutic effect, and this is the case whether we call the process psychoanalysis or psychotherapy. This points to the nature of what is therapeutic within the mind; whatever leads to integration and self-awareness, whatever leads to the truth, is therapeutic. As Symington seems to suggest, 'psychotherapy' based on suggestion is deadly to self-awareness and antithetical to integration, so why call it 'psychotherapy'? Suggestion as a technique is antitherapeutic because it is directed towards reinforcing splitting, that is, towards keeping the 'bad objects' from consciousness. For this reason, it does not seem clarifying to say that techniques of suggestion constitute forms of psychotherapy. To suggest, as Symington does, that one of the 'techniques of healing' employed by psychotherapists is to 'make declarations and allow the inner spirit to be enveloped by them' involves, I believe, a contradiction, in that such techniques do not facilitate healing.

Psychoanalysis and psychotherapy

I have argued that a distinction between psychotherapy and psychoanalysis can only be maintained at the level of convention, and tends to disappear at the level of truth. Ultimately what is psychotherapeutic is the presence of psychoanalytic work between the patient and physician. If a process of 'psychotherapy' is to prove psychotherapeutic, in any more than a serendipitous way, I think this depends on the presence of psychoanalytic work. The presence of psychoanalytic work in the mind of the physician is a necessary but not sufficient condition for this process to develop between patient and physician. Ultimately good enough 'psychoanalysis' is likely to prove psychotherapeutic and a curative force, and conversely the extent to which any 'psychotherapy' can lead to cure is the extent to which a psychoanalytic process can be facilitated within that therapy.

The paradox here is that for the physician to become an effective psychotherapist he or she must relinquish therapeutic zeal. The analytic therapist does not have a preconception that the patient's symptoms and suffering are a bad thing. While the therapist may feel sympathetic to the patient's predicament or distress, he or she maintains a relative impartiality regarding any wish on the patient's behalf for relief from symptoms and suffering. The patient who does not feel free to have his or her symptoms is unlikely to feel free to be cured. As Bion, Symington and others have pointed out, the immediate aim of clinical psychoanalysis is self-awareness through understanding the mind. To the extent that curing of the mind takes place, it is a by-product of this activity of understanding. Paradoxically unless understanding is privileged over relief the potential cure is likely to be compromised.

It would seem important for psychoanalysts to distinguish what they attempt to do from the so-called 'psychotherapies' based on various forms of suggestion; however, I think this is a different question from attempting to distinguish 'psychoanalysis' from 'psychotherapy' in principle. The idea of linking the term psychotherapy with cure by suggestion seems too general, and I think contradicts the reality of what is psychotherapeutic. Rather than attempt to distance 'psychoanalysis' from 'psychotherapy' perhaps psychoanalysts can lay greater claim to the psychotherapeutic effects of psychoanalysis, even if they are 'side effects'.

References

Cervantes, M. de (1986). *Don Quixote de la Mancha.* London: Andre Deutsch. (Original work published 1605).

Symington, N. (2004). The difference between psychotherapy and psychoanalysis. *Psychoanalysis Downunder*, 5. Retrieved from: https://www.psychoanalysisdownunder.com.au/issue-5

Fairbairn, W.R.D. (1990). *Psychoanalytic Studies of the Personality*. London: Routledge. (Original work published 1943).

'In my end is my beginning': T.S. Eliot's *The Waste Land and* after

First published in *The British Journal of Psychotherapy*; Volume 18, Number 3, 2002. 381-399

Abstract

The publication of *The Waste Land* established Eliot's reputation as a major poet. The poem was written out of an experience of emotional 'breakdown', and its innovative free associative form conveys a sense of psychological fragmentation. While Eliot emphasized the necessary distance that must be achieved between personal experience and successful creative expression, all his major poems were written out of periods of personal crisis and growth, and remain intensely personal. This paper explores links between Eliot's personal emotional experience and the poetry. It suggests that for Eliot poetry was part of a journey of self-exploration, and at the time of *The Waste Land* and subsequently, became a vital part of his struggle towards a new integration within his self.

T.S. Eliot's nervous breakdown in 1921 coincided with his completion of *The Waste Land*, and constituted a turning point in his life. A movement towards psychological breakdown can be traced from the time of his first marriage up until the writing of *The Waste Land*, while his subsequent life, at least until his second marriage at age sixty-eight, manifests a slow and painful struggle towards a new integration within his self.

In his paper 'T.S. Eliot and The Waste Land', Harry Trosman (1974) has comprehensively documented the events leading up to Eliot's breakdown, his treatment with the Swiss psychiatrist Dr Roger Vittoz, and his writing of *The Waste Land.* Trosman points out that the poem captures a process of psychic disintegration, and suggests that the writing itself, as part of an attempted reintegration within the poet's self, constituted a form of 'partial self-analytic work.' (1974 p. 717)

Although Eliot took steps to limit the material that would be posthumously available to biographers, two major biographies, Peter Ackroyd's *T.S. Eliot* (1984) and Lyndall Gordon's *T.S. Eliot: An Imperfect Life* (1998), have appeared since the publication of Trosman's paper in 1974. The present paper draws on the currently available biographical information, and Trosman's analysis of the 'psychopathological antecedents and transformations' of *The Waste Land*, in order to further explore the idea of the writing of *The Waste Land* as a form of partial self-analytic work, and to suggest that throughout Eliot's life poetry constituted a vital part of his analytic work towards reintegration within his self.

Eliot was much interested in the question of the relationship between lived experience and poetry, and his critical writings emphasize the distance he felt must be achieved in order for emotional experience to be successfully transformed into a work of art. In his essay 'Tradition and the Individual Talent', he advocated an 'impersonal theory of poetry': '...the more perfect the artist, the more completely separate in him will be the man who suffers and the mind which creates; the more perfectly will the mind digest and transmute the passions which are its material' (1920 p. 54). As Ackroyd (1984) has pointed out, this statement, paradoxically, confirms just how intimately Eliot's passions and suffering were linked to his creative expression. All his major poems are intensely personal and written out of periods of personal crisis and growth.

The truly creative act can be understood as a form of thinking about lived emotional experience. Wilfred Bion saw creative growth as the outcome of the realization and awareness of emotional experience, as represented in his categories of linkage: Love, Hate, Knowledge (in notation L,H,K). Bion believed that growth within the mind depends ultimately upon the presence of the K link, the wish to get to know, which confers the capacity to confront and tolerate the frustration and suffering inherent in the realization of psychic reality (Bion, 1994).

This paper takes as its starting point Eliot's own observation that his passions and suffering constituted the raw materials for his art. It explores how the emergence and realization of emotional experience and, often painful, self-awareness, was linked to his transforming creative expression. It suggests a mutual relationship between the poetry and Eliot's struggle towards integration within his mind. While the paper explores the poetry within the context of these ideas, there is no wish to suggest that the essence of creativity can be reduced to a psychoanalytic theory; as a manifestation of life the creative act remains as mysterious in its essence as life itself.

Background

T.S. Eliot was born in St. Louis, Missouri in 1888, the seventh and last child of Henry Ware Eliot and Charlotte Champe Stearns, both aged forty-five. He was nine years younger than his nearest surviving sibling. Another child had been born in 1886 but died after a few months. The family was Unitarian, and Eliot's paternal grandfather, William Greenleaf Eliot, a Unitarian minister who died shortly before Eliot was born, was a family exemplar of rectitude whose influence continued to dominate from the grave.

Eliot seems also to have experienced his parents as remote figures (Gordon, 1998). Charlotte Eliot was a high-minded woman who, by the time of his birth, was devoting much of her energy to a variety of social causes. She had probably not anticipated another child, although a wish to replace the lost baby cannot be discounted. While her conscious intention was to provide the best for her son, she may have had considerable ambivalence about the demands of motherhood being renewed at forty-five when she had begun to develop a life of her own. In the light of one relative's observation that she was not particularly interested in babies (Ackroyd, 1984 p. 20), it is possible she was not fully available to her son during his first years. He had a nurse as a young child, Annie Dunn, described by Trosman as a 'rigid, Irish Catholic nursemaid' (Trosman, 1974 p. 295), although the picture of their relationship offered by Gordon, and Eliot's comment that he was 'greatly attached' to her (Gordon, 1977 p. 3), suggest a more sympathetic figure.

Charlotte's attitude towards the body was highly ambivalent: 'Purge from thy heart all sensual desire, / Let low ambitions perish in the fire' (Gordon, 1998 p. 163), are lines from one of her own poems, inspired mostly by her religious values and reforming zeal. Having aspired to be a poet she met with little success, and when Eliot's precocious abilities became evident his mother began to hope he would vicariously fulfil her own failed literary ambitions. She wrote to him at Harvard: 'I hope in your literary work you will receive early the recognition I strove for and failed.' (Gordon, 1977 p. 4) In Herbert Howarth's assessment:

> ...the family guessed at an early date that T.S. Eliot has unusual abilities and exerted all their care to foster them and guard him against bruises. Mrs Eliot looked forward to the day when he would take his place in New York among his country's most prominent writers and perform the work she had longed to perform and win the acknowledgment she would have most desired to win.

(Howarth, 1965 p. 33)

Charlotte's tendency to regard him as a young adult is reflected in the letter, she wrote to the headmaster of Milton Academy before his entry into that school at age seventeen. Ackroyd has summarized its content: 'Mrs Eliot explained in a letter… how her son had been deprived of companions of his own age: she was used to talking to him as though he were a man, which was perhaps not good for him.' (Ackroyd, 1984 p. 28)

Henry Ware Eliot chose a career in business and after initial unsuccessful ventures went into brickmaking, becoming president of the Hydraulic-Press Brick Company in St Louis, and relatively wealthy in the process. In justifying his rejection of his own father's ambition that he become a Unitarian minister, Henry Ware Eliot is purported to have said: 'Too much pudding choked the dog.' (Ackroyd, 1984 p. 18) The title of his memoirs; *The Reminiscences of a Simpleton*, suggests a self-deprecatory attitude; he had aspired to be a painter but the fulfilment of this creative ambition remained restricted to his habit of making sketch drawings of cats, and he appears to have regarded his career as in some respects a failure.

Eliot recognized that most of his childhood experience had been constrained by a Puritan family ethic of self-denial. Throughout his life he was unable to buy sweets which he had been taught to regard as needless self-gratification (Ackroyd, 1984). His parents' ideal of sensual mortification included the sexual. According to Gordon, Henry Ware Eliot considered sex 'nastiness', and syphilis as God's punishment for sin. He hoped no cure would be found for this disease, because if it was it might be necessary 'to emasculate our children to keep them clean' (Gordon, 1977 p. 27). To compound the difficulties, Eliot was born with a congenital double hernia. It can hardly be imagined that this socially invisible physical defect, and his consequent need to wear a truss, did not have a profound psychological impact; it constituted a narcissistic injury, and seems to have exacerbated his mother's and sister's tendency to anxious over-protectiveness (Ackroyd, 1984). At an unconscious level it may have represented concrete evidence of parental retribution against unacceptable sexuality. The hernias were not surgically repaired until 1947 when Eliot was 58.

Gordon has suggested that aspects of Eliot's writing reflect a wish to recapture an ideal and 'remarkably happy' early childhood experience (Gordon, 1977 p. 14). While there is a detectable '*nostalgie de l'enfance*' (Ackroyd, 1984 p. 180) it is in the nature of a wish for something insufficiently present, a sense of loss and longing for some ineffable aspect of childhood experience, on the border of consciousness. Biographical details actually suggest Eliot's loneliness as a boy, and the unequivocally happy memories are mostly associated with the sea and summer holidays at Cape Anne, New England.

Although he would fulfil his mother's ambition that he become a successful poet, Eliot's ambivalence about his parents' influence and ideals is readily traced in his life and work. In 1910, after completing his master's degree at Harvard, and influenced by ideas of Symbolism in literature, Eliot left America and his family to spend a year in Paris.

Aboulie

> I have heard the mermaids singing, each to each.
> I do not think that they will sing to me.
>
> (The Love Song of J. Alfred Prufrock)

In Paris he seems to have experienced a sense of emotional isolation, at least from women, and been tormented by frustrated sexual desire (Ackroyd, 1984). He completed his two major early poems, *The Love Song of J. Alfred Prufrock* and *Portrait of a Lady*, which show a self-conscious recognition of the symptom complex he would later diagnose as his 'aboulie'. *Prufrock* opens with its memorable image of unconscious paralysis:

> Let us go then, you and I,
> When the evening is spread out against the sky
> Like a patient etherised upon a table;

We are invited to enter the world of Prufrock's subjective experience in company with his self-observing ego, and Prufrock clearly reflects aspects of Eliot's own self at the time of writing. Prufrock and the protagonist in *Portrait of a Lady* are depicted only in relationship to women; society women who exist in worlds refined and trivial; and with whom they maintain relationships both tenuous and ambivalent. Faced with the enervation consequent upon his emotional detachment, the protagonist in *Portrait of a Lady* seeks to console himself with the satisfactions of his apparently superior sensibility. He is nevertheless half aware of sentiments that cannot safely be verbalized:

> Inside my brain a dull tom-tom begins
> Absurdly hammering a prelude of its own,
> Capricious monotone
> That is at least one definite 'false note'.

This suppressed, primitive, and hostile energy, seems to offer a possibility of definition, but it is an aspect of the inner self that is avoided. In both poems such primitive energies, and desire in relation to the feminine, are held in check, and conversation fails as a vehicle for truth. The portrait of Eliot they suggest is of a man with a well-developed social persona concealing considerable narcissistic vulnerability, and of the loss of vitality and instinctual energy consequent upon the withdrawal of the 'true self'

(Winnicott, 1960). Eliot was at an impasse; he had an intuitive appreciation of his affliction, his 'aboulie', but no idea what the remedy should be.

He returned to America to pursue doctoral studies in philosophy at Harvard and seemed to be heading for an academic career. In 1914 Bertrand Russell, who was visiting professor at Harvard, described the young Eliot as, '... proficient in Plato, intimate with French literature from Villon to Vildrach, very capable of a certain exquisiteness of appreciation, but lacking in the crude insistent passion that one must have in order to achieve anything.' (Clark, 1975 p. 231) Russell's judgment was astute but he could not observe the evidence of a rebellion against self-imposed orthodoxy that was incubating within Eliot.

Eliot took up a travelling fellowship to return to Europe, arriving in England just before the outbreak of war. In London he met Ezra Pound and was introduced to the contemporary literary scene, already one of innovation and experiment. Pound, a successful fellow American, championed Eliot and his work, asserting confidently that he would become a major poet. Pound's eccentricity and extroversion challenged Eliot's conformity and introversion, and it seems, as Trosman (1974) and Edel (1982) have speculated, that Pound's influence on the direction Eliot's life was to follow was considerable.

In 1915 Eliot met Vivien Haigh-Wood and two months later the couple were married. She was attractive, vivacious, and intelligent, with a keen dramatic sense. As an embodiment of an energizing and exciting feminine principle, she seemed to offer the promise of liberation. Eliot, however, had been unable to perceive the extreme emotional vulnerability and dependence that lay beneath Vivien's extrovert social persona.

'Memory and desire'

April is the cruellest month, breeding
Lilacs out of the dead land, mixing
Memory and desire, stirring
Dull roots with spring rain.
Winter kept us warm, covering
Earth in forgetful snow…

The Waste Land—Part I. The Burial of the Dead (l 1–6)

The importance of the sexual attraction in facilitating Eliot's marriage is suggested in his comment, written a year afterwards: 'For the boy whose childhood has been empty of beauty, who has never known the *detached* curiosity for beauty, who's been brought up to see goodness as practical and to take the line of self-interest in a code of rewards and punishments, then the sexual instinct when it is aroused may mean the only possible escape from a prosaic world.' (Gordon, 1977 p. 72) Gordon has commented, 'Eliot married quickly on the crest of a moment of rapport… It was almost necessary for Eliot to act impulsively—to forestall habitual scruples—if he were to act at all.' (ibid. p. 74)

In his hope for a new freedom Eliot was to be disappointed. In a much-quoted passage Bertrand Russell wrote to Ottoline Morrell, 'she (Vivien) says she married him to stimulate him, but finds she can't do it. Obviously, he married in order to be stimulated. I think she will soon be tired of him.' (Russell, 1968 p. 54) (Russell's comments should be interpreted in the context that he was soon to begin an affair with Vivien (Gordon, 1998 p. 121)). Ultimately the couple's emotional difficulties and incompatibilities would prove beyond their capacity to resolve, but they struggled on together until Eliot finally left Vivien in 1933. As Ackroyd (1984 p. 85) has commented, 'it would be wrong to underestimate the bonds between Eliot and Vivien even in the midst of their difficulties.'

From the outset the marriage constituted an enormous strain for both parties. Eliot experienced bouts of exhaustion and depression, while Vivien was increasingly subject to severe episodes of anxiety and depression, as well as a variety of hypochondriacal preoccupations, and physical illnesses (Ackroyd, 1984), probably substantially psychosomatic in origin.

Eliot had married without seeking his parents' approval, a radical departure from family tradition. To their further disapproval, he was considering giving up his doctoral studies. With the express purpose of explaining himself to his parents he travelled, alone, to America. The meeting did not go well, and Eliot left feeling that he had failed to close the rift that had been opened. Objective evidence that the estrangement was real is found in the fact that his father changed the terms of his will so that his son's inheritance was 'in trust' only and not left outright, as to Eliot's siblings. It would revert to the family upon his death (Eliot V., 1971). Back in London Eliot was forced to seek employment, and eventually took a job in Lloyd's bank, where he would remain for nine years.

In 1919 Henry Ware Eliot died. The loss was complicated by the guilt Eliot felt consequent upon his estrangement from his father. He had hoped to effect a reconciliation by becoming a successful poet and was working towards the publication of his first book of poems. After his father's death he wrote, it, '...does not weaken the need for a book at all—it really reinforces it. My mother is still alive.' (Eliot V., 1971 p. xvi)

In the period of mourning Eliot wished intensely to see his mother. In 1920 he wrote, 'I am thinking all the time of my desire to see her. I cannot get away from it. Unless I can really *see* her again, I shall never be happy.' (Eliot V., 1971 p. xviii), and in 1921 Charlotte Eliot along with Eliot's sister Marian and brother Henry visited him in England. Vivien, who had recently been seriously ill, spent most of their visit recuperating in a country cottage.

Probably the animosity between herself and Charlotte (Ackroyd, 1984 p. 111) was the real reason for her absence. Rather than reassure Eliot, the family reunion proved extremely stressful, and his mental health began to deteriorate from the time of their leaving. He wrote, '...I really feel very shaky, and seem to have gone down rapidly since my family left.' (Eliot V., 1971 p. xxi) Eliot consulted a neurologist who diagnosed 'nerves' and prescribed three months rest.

An attempted rest cure of several weeks in Margate was not sufficient, and, on the recommendation of Lady Ottoline Morrell, Eliot travelled to Lausanne to receive treatment from a psychiatrist, Dr Roger Vittoz. Vittoz's methods were non-analytic and involved helping his patient develop a sense of personal integrity and efficacy through a variety of interventions ostensibly focused on regaining control of thought and behaviour. Trosman comments, 'He saw his method as opposed to psychoanalysis. He had no interest in understanding unconscious processes which he believed endangered the unity and integration he attempted to bring about.' (1974 p. 713) Trosman documents Vittoz treatment of cerebral 'reeducation', which began with exercises involving concentration on sensations without thought. Exercises of graduated complexity involving attention and concentration upon ideas were introduced, and finally the patient was 'taught to exercise the will and given lessons in how to use it.' (1974 p. 713) Throughout there was emphasis on calm and rest, and the treatment involved much personal contact with Vittoz who believed he could feel his patients' brainwaves by placing his hand upon their foreheads. In so doing he assessed the extent of disordered cerebral functioning and monitored the progress of treatment. Patients found him 'an exceptionally gentle and saintly person.' (Trosman, 1974 p. 713) Eliot liked and trusted Vittoz, and it seems there was a degree of idealization towards this paternal figure. The approach was helpful; Eliot felt better and was able to complete his draft of *The Waste Land,* which had been under way at least since the beginning of 1921.

In January 1922 Eliot submitted his manuscript, probably for the second time (Gordon, 1998), to the critical eye of Ezra Pound. Pound now suggested editorial revision, particularly the omission of sections he considered weakened the overall effect, and for the most part Eliot accepted the revisions. What Pound referred to as his 'Caesarean Operation' sharpened the focus and improved the poem.

The Waste Land

In its final published version, the poem is in five sections of varying length, content, and style. Eliot's original title, *He Do the Police in Different Voices*, taken from Charles Dickens's *Our Mutual Friend*, reflects the polyphonic intention of the poem, and the way in which apparently disparate parts or fragments are united into a whole. As well as the narrating voice of the poet/persona, many other voices and characters speak their own lines or make brief appearances. Eliot sets out to capture 'demotic' language and the contemporary scene, as in an episode in Part III, *The Fire Sermon*, where a 'young man carbuncular' engages in an act of automatic sexual intercourse with a 'typist home at teatime.' After *The Waste Land* was published many commentators focused on its depiction of contemporary life, offering interpretations of the poem as a rejection of the values of the fragmented wasteland of contemporary Western culture, and as a critique of the emotional alienation suffered by its members. Such interpretations became commonplace and Eliot was moved to issue a disclaimer of his poem as a social critique: 'To me it was only the relief of a personal and wholly insignificant grouse against life; it is just a piece of rhythmical grumbling.' (Eliot V., 1971 p. 1)

If, as Eliot invites us to do, we read the poem as a statement of the poet's self, the fragmented wasteland becomes an internal reality, revealed in the 'objective correlatives' (Eliot, 1920 p. 100), to use Eliot's own term, of the scenes and images of the poem.

The opening lines of Part I, *The Burial of the Dead* (quoted above), communicate resistance to the thawing life force of spring, mixing 'memory and desire'. The 'dead land' of inner objects and of desire within the old self, is stirring to life, creating the possibility of breakdown; 'fear in a handful of dust' (l 30), but also the possibility of a new beginning: 'That corpse you planted last year in your garden, / 'Has it begun to sprout? Will it bloom this year? (l 71–2)

Written after the disillusion and sexual failure of his marriage, the death of his father, and the failure of reconciliation with his mother, the poem contains no portrayal of a satisfactory love relationship. The encounter with the idealized 'hyacinth girl' is desired but 'my eyes failed, I was neither / Living nor dead, and I knew nothing' (l 39–40). The encounter which remains, and takes place in a land of 'dry stone' with 'no sound of water' (l 24), is essentially with one's self, and the shadow of one's self: 'Your shadow at morning striding behind you / Or your shadow at evening rising to meet you' (l 28–9).

Part II, *A Game of Chess*, suggests an anxious interlude and the wish to defer breakdown. The passage and pressure of time is felt and heard 'HURRY UP PLEASE ITS TIME' (l 141), but there are various devices, 'a closed car at four' and 'a game of chess' (l 136–7), which might be employed to further its eventless passage. Central to part II is the devastating portrait of failed communication between an introspective ineffectual man and an agitated near hysterical woman. While these lines achieve the necessary 'impersonality', the experience of Eliot's marriage was essential to their composition.

In Part III, *The Fire Sermon,* 'The river's tent is broken' (l 173), and movement restored: 'Sweet Thames, run softly till I end my song' (l 183).

Eliot probably wrote the draft of part III in Margate during the unsuccessful rest cure, then completed it in Lausanne on the shores of Lake Geneva (Lac Leman) where he received treatment from Vittoz (Gordon 1998 p. 172). In *The Fire Sermon* Eliot makes his personal emotional crisis explicit by reference to his state of self-fragmentation and alienation: 'On Margate Sands. / I can connect / Nothing with nothing.' (l 300–2) But *The Fire Sermon* also identifies Lausanne as the place where inner connection can occur: 'By the waters of Leman I sat down and wept...' (l 182). The presence of water is linked to movement and release.

In counterpoint is the 'fire' motif. The 'human engine' (l 216) that brings the sexual encounters, 'Sweeny to Mrs Porter' (l 198), and the young man to the typist, is also a combustion engine, like 'a taxi throbbing waiting' (l 217). Immediately after the point of recognition of self-fragmentation; 'I can connect / Nothing with nothing', the poet identifies himself with St Augustine, 'Burning burning burning burning' (l 308), in the 'cauldron of unholy loves' that Augustine describes in his *Confessions* (see Eliot's Notes to *The Waste Land*), and places himself at the mercy of the Lord.

The persona who narrates the sexual encounter between typist and young man is the mythological and androgynous figure Tiresias:

> (And I Tiresias have foresuffered all
> Enacted on this same divan or bed;
> I who have sat by Thebes below the wall
> And walked among the lowest of the dead.) (l 243–6)

Like Tiresias who encompasses all, Eliot's purpose is to avow, rather than disavow, a common humanity with typist and clerk. Their forced intercourse is the 'objective correlative' of a psychic state where true emotional links (L,H,K) cannot be realized. Tiresias' blindness suggests that such links must be created from within and discerned with an inner vision. In parallel, the links between what appear initially as the disparate and discontinuous elements of *The Waste Land*, emerge at a deeper level through the free association of image and symbol, and in 'the music' of the poetry (Eliot 1957).

Part IV, *Death by Water*, is short but rich in associations, and seems to suggest a possibility for redemption in renunciation of the existing and worldly self, and an attitude of humility in the face of death; a death by water not fire. Both part IV and V were written in Lausanne.

The fifth and final section, *What the Thunder Said,* has been described by Stephen Spender as 'visionary poetry written out of intense suffering and transforms the poet into seer.' (Spender, 1975 p. 112) In the barren aridity of the wasteland all existence longs for water, 'But there is no water' (l 358). Thunder can be heard but it is 'dry sterile thunder without rain' (l 342). Then, miraculously, a flash of lightening, and 'a damp gust / Bringing rain' (l 393–4). The thunder is heard again, but no longer sterile, it 'speaks' three times. The persona/poet interprets the voice of the thunder as the injunctions: 'Datta, Dayadhvam, Damyata'; Sanskrit words translated by Eliot in his notes to the poem as: 'Give, Sympathise, Control'.

The moral injunctions of the thunder suggest the presence of a benign paternal authority, but outside the sphere of human relationship. The apparent movement in *The Waste Land* is away from the limitations and failure of human love towards the possibility of spiritual redemption.

Following the moments of truth communicated by the thunder, the final stanza offers a series of loosely, or freely, associated lines in several languages, bound together in an incantatory rhythm. There is explicit acknowledgment that the poem represents an attempt to maintain integration of the self in the face of threatened or partial disintegration: 'These fragments have I shored against my ruins' (l 430), but nevertheless 'Hieronymo's mad againe' (l 431). The poem ends in the repetition 'Shantih shantih shantih' (l 433), another Sanskrit word which Eliot's notes identify as the formal end to an Upanishad; and translate as: 'The Peace which passeth understanding.'

Trosman has suggested that the symptoms of Eliot's breakdown; depression with exhaustion, indecisiveness, hypochondriasis, and fear of psychosis; were manifestations of a temporary disintegration of ego functioning in a narcissistically vulnerable personality. He identifies the death of Eliot's father as of 'paramount importance in terms of Eliot's psychological stability' (Trosman, 1974 p. 712), and the sense of estrangement and alienation Eliot experienced following the failure of his mother's visit, occurring within the context of the failure of his marriage, as the significant precipitant for his decompensation. Employing the concept of the self-object, Trosman formulates that following a 'failure in response from need-satisfying and narcissistically cathected self-objects, he found himself empty, fragmented, and lacking in a sense of self-cohesion.' (1974 p. 717) It seems, as Trosman suggests, that Eliot found Vittoz a suitable figure for idealization and that their co-operative engagement in the therapeutic endeavour contributed to his self-stabilization and regaining a sense of self cohesion. Trosman points out that because Vittoz could not provide Eliot with insight into the nature of his disorder, the treatment remained essentially supportive and limited, although the writing of *The Waste Land* may have constituted 'a form of partial self-analytic work' (1974 p. 717).

While the treatment with Vittoz appeared to aim for self-stabilization, and might be considered as essentially palliative, an examination of *The Waste Land* itself, and of Eliot's creative process at the time of writing, suggests that much more was taking place within his mind than the restoration of defences and the regaining of self-control.

What the Thunder Said was written in Lausanne during the treatment with Vittoz, and Eliot told Virginia Woolf that he wrote this final section of the poem in a trance. In a later interview he commented, 'I wasn't even bothering whether I understood what I was saying' (Ackroyd, 1984 p. 116). Eliot was surely reflecting upon this experience when, in *The Use of Poetry and the Use of Criticism,* he makes an analogy between mystical experience and some of the ways poetry is written:

> 'I know, for instance, that some forms of ill-health, debility or anemia, may (if other circumstances are favourable) produce an efflux of poetry in a way approaching the condition of automatic writing.... What one writes in this way... gives me the impression... of having undergone a long incubation, though we do not know until the shell breaks what kind of egg we have been sitting on. To me it seems that at these moments, which are characterised by the sudden lifting of the burden of anxiety and fear which presses upon our daily life so steadily that we are unaware of it, what happens is something *negative*: that is to say, not 'inspiration' as we commonly think of it, but the breaking down of strong habitual barriers—which tend to re-form very quickly.' (Eliot, 1933 p. 144) ('ill-health, debility, or anemia,' readily translate as 'aboulie'.)

'Anxiety and fear' may be considered as passive registers, or signals, of emotional experience. *What the Thunder Said* was able to hatch, more or less fully formed after long incubation, as a result of the 'breaking down of strong habitual barriers', or defences, allowing the transformation of emotional experience to an active register; using Bion's terms there was experience in the domain L,H,K. The process of psychic fragmentation taking place within Eliot appears to have been a necessary precondition for this experience to be realized, and the supportive nature of Vittoz's treatment appears to have contained anxiety to a point where a creative synthesis could take place. Eliot said that, as a result of the treatment, he felt calmer than he had for a long time, likening this calmness to that he had known as a child (Ackroyd, 1984 p. 116). The poem itself reflects this process of the formation of emotional links and understanding, the recognition of loss, and the cathartic experience of grief: 'By the waters of Leman I sat down and wept' (l 182). Significantly, Pound did not find it necessary to suggest major changes to *What the Thunder Said.*

While Vittoz acted as a benign paternal transference figure with whom Eliot was able to identify, the transference can also be conceptualized in terms of a maternal holding experience. The trust Eliot felt towards Vittoz relieved fragmentation anxiety and allowed a transitional space of relatedness within which he could contain the cathartic upwelling and creative synthesis of 'unconscious' elements. This dimension of Eliot's experience is suggested in the arrival of life-giving rain in the wasteland. The paternal voice of the thunder announces or brings the rain, but the engendering of new life in the earth also suggests the maternal function. There is a creative union, restoring at least a partial vitality to the wasteland.

Beyond 'Memory and desire'

> We shall not cease from exploration
> And the end of all our exploring
> Will be to arrive where we started
> And know the place for the first time.
>
> *Little Gidding—Four Quartets*)

Eliot noted that the 'strong habitual barriers' within his mind tended to reform quickly, however the experience of breakdown at the time of *The Waste Land* was profound, precluding a complete restoration of old and habitual defences, and the analytic work of the poem was insufficient to achieve a new integration. Eliot's self, like London Bridge (*The Waste Land,* l 426) was to remain in danger of collapse for some years. 'I am worn out,

I cannot go on', he wrote to John Quinn in 1923 (Eliot V., 1971 p. xxvii). *The Hollow Men* (1925), Eliot's next major poem, is perhaps the fullest expression of his ongoing sense of impotence and paralysis:

> Between the emotion
> And the response
> Falls the Shadow

The shadow; the dark side of the self, is directly implicated in the state of paralysis. *The Hollow Men* was written following a second visit by Eliot's mother to England in 1924, perhaps in response to a renewed experience of inner emptiness and guilt. The poem concludes, 'This is the way the world ends / Not with a bang but a whimper'; suggesting the turning inward or exhaustion of potentially explosive infantile rage in the face of an experience of intolerable helplessness, and a turning away from the mother/other. The world of the poem is one of the complete failures of relationship, but it is also a world of the suspension of passionate or instinctual energy, where there are no 'lost / Violent souls,' but only 'hollow men'.

The content of the poem is stark and shattering, but the recognition of truth is a precondition for change, and a tenuous hope is communicated. The poetry itself serves to affirm the reality of the experience, while the incantatory rhythms, reminiscent of the liturgy, and the fragments of the Lord's prayer in part V, point the direction Eliot was moving in his attempt to be reconciled with the emptiness and the shadows within: in 1927 he was baptized and confirmed in the Church of England.

Eliot's religious conversion can be interpreted as part of his attempt to shore up the 'ruin' of his self through renunciation of the uncertain possibilities of human love in favour of the redemption and security offered in a relationship with the spiritual. Trosman (1977 p. 303) speculates that in response to his fears of a 'psychotic merger' with his wife and a 'return to the hypochondriacal fragmentation characteristic of his illness at the time of the composition of *The Waste Land*' Eliot, 'turned more and more to a system of beliefs which would make intelligible his inner turmoil and provide the sense of unity he so sorely lacked'. This movement, and the accompanying repudiation of sexuality, referred to by Gordon as 'Eliot's vow of celibacy' (Gordon, 1998 p. 312) found fullest expression in his 'conversion' poem, *Ash Wednesday* (1930).

Part I opens with insistence at having arrived at a point to obviate hope:

Because I do not hope to turn again
Because I do not hope
Because I do not hope to turn

The usual objects of worldly pursuit, 'this man's gift and that man's scope,' are renounced, and the repudiation of sexual desire is implicit. As Chouinard (1971) has pointed out, the 'anima' representation in *Ash Wednesday* has become that of the Virgin Mary, the 'silent sister'.

In part II Eliot writes of, 'The greater torment / Of love satisfied', than the 'torment / Of love unsatisfied', and thus, at the end of part II, comes to the point of renunciation of human love, and acceptance of division and disunity. If unity is possible it is so only in spiritual love, and the poem ends in part VI with a plea for such unity.

Even among these rocks,
Our peace in His will
And even among these rocks
Sister, mother
And spirit of the river, spirit of the sea,
Suffer me not to be separated
And let my cry come unto Thee.

Eliot was unwilling to 'cease from exploration', and so in the end unable to avoid psychic pain. Like the treatment with Vittoz, Eliot's religious conversion can be conceptualized in its defensive and self-stabilizing aspects, and at the same time as providing a framework which helped him contain and realize his emotional experience. The system of belief that he now embraced, by conferring meaning and value to suffering, helped render suffering bearable. Implicit in the final lines of *Ash Wednesday* is a hope, that through the realization of the pain of separation, separation might ultimately be transcended. The poem suggests the possibility that Eliot's religious conversion fulfilled a transitional function to that end.

Charlotte Eliot had died in 1929, leaving her son again guilty and anguished as a consequence of their incomplete reconciliation (Ackroyd, 1984 p. 178). Vivien Eliot had become increasingly incapacitated in her physical and psychological health, showing a disposition towards paranoia, manifest as pathological jealousy, and probably frank psychosis. The couple's relationship was increasingly estranged, and in 1933 Eliot left his wife. Perhaps because of his guilt he did not forewarn her of his intention, and for many years she continued to believe that he would finally return to her. Vivien was eventually committed to a psychiatric hospital for involuntary treatment.

Eliot acted as a fire warden in London during World War II, and his response to the blitz found expression in *Little Gidding*, the last of *Four Quartets*. After the war he took up residence with John Hayward, a man of forceful personality, but also a cripple and confined to a wheelchair. Ackroyd (1984 p. 278) comments that the essential feature of the life which Eliot constructed for himself was that it 'contained as few surprises as possible.' In an anecdote from this period W.H. Auden recalled asking Eliot why he liked playing the card game patience so much. 'Well, I suppose it's the nearest thing to being dead', Eliot is said to have replied (Spender, 1975 p. 240). However, Gordon's recent (1998) biography makes clear just how much was taking place beneath the apparently smooth surface of Eliot's life of waiting. In particular she reveals the full importance of Eliot's ongoing relationship over many years with an American woman, Emily Hale, the 'hyacinth girl' of *The Waste Land* (1 36); an embodiment of the possibility of ideal but unrealized romantic love. Their relationship went back to 1912, and it is clear that Emily Hale spent much of her life waiting for Eliot. When Vivien died in 1947, Hale hoped that he was finally free to marry her and certainly Eliot too had considered this possibility. In the end, he could not (Gordon, 1998 p. 411).

Poetry and self analysis

The evidence suggests that Eliot's supportive treatment with Vittoz, while limited in scope, facilitated the creative movement within the self manifest in *The Waste Land.* While Vittoz did not encourage insight, he could not preclude it. In the light of Eliot's comments in *The Music of Poetry,* that 'There may be much more in a poem than the author was aware of' (Eliot, 1957 p. 31), and 'the poet is occupied with frontiers of consciousness beyond which words fail, though meanings still exist' (1957 p. 30), it seems likely that Eliot was able to return to, and gain insight into, what had been written 'in a trance' without conscious understanding.

Eliot's breakdown and the writing of *The Waste Land* represented a turning point in his life. Through the loss and rupture of stabilizing relationships, Eliot was thrown back upon himself, and upon his capacity for self-examination. Movement from a state of relatively stable psychic integration to one of unintegration (in Bion's notation movement D → PS (Bion, 1984)), is the precondition for the emergence of a new state of integration (PS → D2). Eliot's journey of exploration after *The Waste Land* can be interpreted in terms of his need to confront the state of emotional isolation and inner emptiness depicted in *The Hollow Men*, and the slow struggle for a new emotional integration within his self.

Although Eliot's attitude to psychoanalytic thought was ambivalent (Gordon, 1998 pp. 200, 479), he possessed a clear conception of the existence within himself of powerful unconscious processes. Ackroyd (1984 p. 20) documents that after his mother's death, Eliot taught contemporary literature at Harvard, and details how Eliot, 'told his students there that D.H. Lawrence had, in *Fantasia of the Unconscious*, written with more acumen about "mother love" than any psychologist.' Ackroyd summarizes Lawrence's argument, 'that the idealized love of a mother for her son can nourish the intellectual and spiritual development of the child at the expense of his sensuality and independence.' Eliot's poetry after *The Hollow Men* manifests his concern with establishing a spiritual and intellectual foundation for life, and his need for a stable 'system of beliefs' (Trosman, 1977 p. 303) on which he could depend. However, alongside this, and linked to the 'music' of the poetry, a latent movement can be discerned culminating in *Four Quartets*, with their elaboration of a truly independent philosophy, and their expression of a new-found sensuality. Poetry was a vital part of Eliot's self-analytic work in the service of restoring the balance between his intellectual and spiritual life, and his sensuality and independence of mind.

Four Quartets, Eliot's last major poetical work and last innovation of form, explores philosophical and spiritual concerns, at times of considerable abstraction, while retaining a powerful capacity to emotionally engage the reader. The work addresses universal concerns which transcend individual particulars, apparently seeking freedom from the tyranny of the personal self and of time.

This is the use of memory:
For liberation—not less of love but expanding
Of love beyond desire, and so liberation
From future as well as past.

(*Little Gidding*)

The poet reaches into his self, and in finding, or creating, a still centre of acceptance there, reconciliation becomes possible. 'I said to my soul, be still, and wait without hope' (*East Coker*), but hope is implicit in the act of waiting. Such are the paradoxes that must be tolerated if meaning is to be apprehended: 'Only through time time is conquered' (*Burnt Norton*).

In these complex and subtle poems meaning is inherent in form, shape, and music, as much as any specific content. Their form reflects the possibilities for psychological integration that they seek to explore. Ackroyd has commented of *Burnt Norton* that, 'the only "truth" to be discovered is the formal unity of the poem itself.' (Ackroyd, 1984 p. 230) Alongside and within the philosophical abstractions are images and passages of striking sensuality which convey a quickening of life; an apparent inner freedom born of acceptance. As the tyranny of the personal self has lessened, the attitude of renunciation seems correspondingly lessened. The poet's energies are again more directly engaged in the spheres of ordinary human relationship and activity.

The Music of Poetry

Only by the form, the pattern,
Can words or music reach
The stillness

(*Burnt Norton—Four Quartets*)

Renunciation was not to have the final word. In 1957, at the age of sixty-eight, T.S. Eliot married for the second time. His wife, Valerie Fletcher, was thirty. Eight years earlier she had obtained the post of his personal secretary, and the formal security of their work relationship allowed a gradual intimacy to develop (Ackroyd, 1984). The marriage was the second turning point, transforming and rejuvenating Eliot; even his physical health improved. 'I'm the luckiest man in the world' (Ackroyd, 1984 p. 321), he declared with uncharacteristic openness.

During the remaining eight years of his life the couple were inseparable. Eliot rejoiced in the new-found happiness and held on to life tenaciously in the face of chronic physical illness. In an interview after his death Valerie Eliot stated: 'He obviously needed to have a happy marriage. He couldn't die until he had had it. There was ... a little boy in him that had never been released.' (Ackroyd, 1984 p. 320) As Edel (1982) has suggested, the security of his second marriage allowed Eliot to come to terms with 'time past' and 'time future'. His last published poem, *A Dedication to my Wife,* was placed initially in front of his last play *The Elder Statesman,* with a final version contained in the *Collected Poems: 1909–1962.* It finds a new voice of freedom and rebirth in 'time present':

> To whom I owe the leaping delight
> That quickens my senses in our wakingtime
> And the rhythm that governs the repose of our sleepingtime,
>   The breathing in unison
> Of lovers whose bodies smell of each other
> Who think the same thoughts without need of speech
> And babble the same speech without need of meaning.

That the 'lovers' of the poem are also mother and infant seems inescapable. To enter into the merged relationship with the other of the poem, the will to individual definition and the assertion of meaning in words must be relinquished. In this new communication, akin to the babbling of infant with mother, meaning is reciprocity and rhythm more than content. The poem suggests that the acceptance and mirroring Eliot experienced in his relationship with Valerie Fletcher offered him a direct and alive satisfaction of deep unmet infant needs. Apart from this dedicatory poem Eliot apparently wrote no further significant poetry after his second marriage.

That Eliot should have chosen poetry as a means of self-expression can be understood in terms of his identification with his mother's ideals and ambitions, but it also seems that the 'music of poetry' was the symbolic means by which Eliot represented and attempted to recapture a sensual merger that was felt to be lost. Wright (1991), following Winnicott, has provided a model for the emergence of consciousness as a consequence of the inevitable development of a space between mother and infant, a transitional space which is necessary if the symbolic function of language is to develop. In the suspension of this space carnal knowledge of objects becomes visual knowledge and the possibility of the symbolic function of naming is initially created through the agency of the mother. So too in the mirror of the mother's gaze the self as subjective object can be apprehended and named. Thus 'the word is the reward for abstinence' (Wright, 1991 p. 135), and 'we could guess that the creative word is in direct descent from the symbiotic mother who closely adapted to her child's needs; as though the child, in its use of language, has tried to re-create that lost sense of oneness with the mother.' (1991 p. 139) Wright emphasizes the importance of the good enough adaptation of the mother, and the inevitable subsequent loss or absence of this symbiosis, in facilitating the ordinary acquisition of creative language. But what about the extraordinary acquisition of creative language? Perhaps for Eliot the 'symbiotic mother' was too quickly lost, and through the mother's idealized investment in language, words prematurely became the signifiers, and sanctioned means, by which the child could cross the gulf that had opened in transitional space.

Ackroyd describes Eliot as a 'solitary, curious child peering at the beauty of small things' (1984 p. 23), and Eliot's own childhood memories convey a quality of separateness and loss. Ackroyd documents what might be regarded as a screen memory: Eliot recalled growing up living next to a girls' school. Because of the high wall that separated the school he could hear the sound of the girls' voices, but he could not see them. When he thought they had left he would sometimes venture through a door in the wall and wander through the school, until one day he arrived too soon and found a group of girls staring at him through a window. He fled (1984 p. 22).

Eliot's poetry is riven with a sense of abstinence and gaze across a space or distance; a space which it seems can only be traversed with language, and we begin to approach the carnal and sensual through the music of that language. Often it is the music of Eliot's poetry, like the distant sound of the girls' voices, that provides the link between separate and apparently disparate elements or fragments. Ultimately the very sound and rhythms of the lines carry an essence of meaning, seeming to capture a deeper wish; to leave the realm of communication with words across the space between the self and other, and return to the realm of the felt oneness of sensual merger; where the boundary between self and other might be, for a moment, obliterated.

Even in *The Hollow Men* where the content of the poem suggests nothing but despair, the longed-for union is still felt in the music of the lines. Only in Eliot's last poem, *A Dedication to my Wife*, could the wish to 'babble the same speech without need of meaning' be known and expressed in the manifest content of the poem, as well as finding latent expression in the music of the poetry. Eliot had arrived at the beginning.

References

Ackroyd P. (1984). *T.S. Eliot.* London: Hamish Hamilton.

Bion, W.R. (1984). *Elements of Psychoanalysis.* London: Karnac.

——— (1994). *Learning from Experience.* London: Jason Aronson.

Chouinard, T. (1971). Eliot's 'Oeuvre', Bradley's 'Finite Centres', and Jung's Anima Concept. In *Journal of Analytic Psychology* 16:48–68.

Clark, R.W. (1975). *The Life of Bertrand Russell.* London: Jonathon Cape & Weidenfeld & Nicholson.

Edel, L. (1982). *Stuff of Sleep and Dreams: Experiments in Literary Psychology.* New York: Avon Books.

Eliot, T.S. (1920). *The Sacred Wood: Essays on Poetry and Criticism.* London: Methuen and Co.

——— (1933). *The Use of Poetry and the Use of Criticism.* London: Faber and Faber.

——— (1957). *On Poetry and Poets.* London: Faber and Faber.

——— (1963). *Collected Poems 1909–1962.* London: Faber and Faber.

——— (1971). *The Waste Land—A Facsimile and Transcript of the Original Drafts Including the Annotations of Ezra Pound.* V. Eliot (Ed.). London: Faber and Faber.

Gordon, L. (1977). *Eliot's Early Years.* Oxford: Oxford University Press.

——— (1998). *T. S. Eliot: An Imperfect Life.* London: Vintage Books.

Howarth, H. (1965). *Notes on Some Figures Behind T.S. Eliot.* London: Chatto & Windus.

Russell, B. (1968). *The Autobiography of Bertrand Russell—Volume 2: 1914–1944.* London: George Allen and Unwin.

Spender, S. (1975). *Eliot.* Glasgow: Fontana-Collins.

Trosman, H. (1974). T.S. Eliot and *The Waste Land*: Psychopathological antecedents and transformations. *Archives General Psychiatry* 30:709–717.

——— (1977). After *The Waste Land:* Psychological factors in the religious conversion of T.S. Eliot. *International Review of Psycho-Analysis* 4:295–304.

Winnicott, D.W. (1990). *The Maturational Process and the Facilitating Environment* (pp. 140–152). London: Karnac, (Original work published 1960).

Wright, K. (1991). *Vision and Separation: Between Mother and Baby.* London: Free Association Books.

Freud's 'selected fact': his journey of mourning

Published in *International Journal of Psychoanalysis*, 2018. 99(1), 208-229.

'Insight such as this falls to one's lot but once in a lifetime', wrote Sigmund Freud in his preface to the 1932, third English edition of *The interpretation of dreams* (1900 p. xxxii). Freud's masterpiece documented overwhelming evidence for the symbolic meaning of dreams and set out the metapsychological formulations that would become known as his 'topographical' theory of mind. However, Freud was not one to be satisfied with 'once in a lifetime' and would continue to produce works offering startling new insights into the human mind. One of these texts would be 'Mourning and melancholia', published in 1917. This transformative paper offered an outline of a new metapsychology, and marked a 'paradigm shift' in the still young discipline of psychoanalysis; a shift that would constitute the basis for what Meltzer has termed 'the Kleinian development' (1978), and, as Ogden (2005) has identified, contained the origins of contemporary 'object relations theory'.

Freud coined the term 'metapsychology', presumably as an allusion to metaphysics, to refer to his psychological metatheory; his attempt to abstract an over-arching theory of the mind. In 1915 he began writing a series of papers, originally intended to be a book, that would come to be known as the papers on metapsychology, and which seemed to reflect a wish to review and clarify existing theoretical formulations. As biographer Peter Gay has noted, having written his planned twelve papers, Freud seemed to become dissatisfied, 'holding back, apparently unable to master some lingering dissatisfaction' (1988 p. 367). The first three papers, 'Instincts and their vicissitudes' (1915a), 'Repression' (1915b), and 'The unconscious' (1915c), were duly published in 1915. Freud's mood for reviewing and reiterating his theory then moved, around the end of 1915, to his composition of the 'Introductory lectures on psychoanalysis' (1916–17). However, his preoccupation remained his book on metapsychology (Gay, 1988 p. 369), and a further two of the twelve papers were published in 1917, but then no more. One of these two was 'Mourning and melancholia,' written early in 1915. The remainder of the original twelve papers were almost certainly destroyed by Freud.

While it is grouped with the other metapsychological papers, 'Mourning and melancholia' stands alone, because in it Freud not so much reviews and clarifies existing theoretical concepts, but embarks on a new direction of exploration. Gay speculates that Freud destroyed the remaining seven papers in the series because, 'The foundations that Freud had intended to lay down definitively for his adherents and against his rivals were shifting in his hands' (1988 p. 373). Although Gay does not link his assessment to 'Mourning and melancholia', of the surviving metapsychological papers this is the one which opens up a new direction of inquiry and conveys this sense of shifting foundations. Rather than being grouped with the other papers on metapsychology, 'Mourning and melancholia' is more appropriately grouped with several other short papers written in 1915: 'The disillusionment of war' and 'Our attitude towards death', published together as 'Thoughts for the times on war and death' (1915d), and 'On transience' (1916). Read alongside 'Mourning and melancholia' these three papers offer insight into Freud's emotional experience at the time and suggest further understandings of his new direction.

The present paper will attempt to link shifts in Freud's thinking and theory to his personal emotional journey. It will be argued that Freud's insights into the nature of melancholia and of mourning were accurate and transformative, because they were grounded in his personal and transformative experiences of mourning. Three rather different experiences of mourning will be considered in terms of their impact on Freud's theory and thinking, up until 1915. First, Freud's abandonment, in 1895, of the highly mechanistic and concretized metapsychology of his *Project for a scientific psychology*. Second, Freud's mourning following the death of his father in 1896, which provided the emotional impetus for his self-analysis and *The interpretation of dreams*, along with the formulation of his 'topographical model'; and third, a period of mourning following the outbreak of the First World War, which seemed to precipitate the far reaching reformulations of 'Mourning and melancholia'.

The paper will also argue that not only does 'Mourning and melancholia' offer new and transformative metapsychological formulations, but in it Freud was able to achieve a new integration between his clinical and metapsychological thinking. Freud's text demonstrates his attempting to think afresh, beginning with careful observation of the field. Rather than trying to fit the phenomena of melancholia and mourning into his existing metapsychological concepts, Freud returns to 'first principles', building new conceptual arguments from the clinical ground up. The result is that when he moves toward metapsychological formulation, these formulations remain linked to observed clinical facts, and retain a quality of emerging from his initial observational hypotheses as logically valid inferences, or necessary conclusions.

Wilfred Bion has differentiated two forms of thinking available to the human mind: the integrative thinking necessary for the apprehension of what he termed the 'selected fact' (1962 p. 72), and the rational and logical thinking necessary for the construction of a valid 'scientific deductive system'. However, a 'scientific deductive system' must initially be derived from an accumulation of 'selected fact' experiences (1962 p. 73). A metapsychology constitutes a 'scientific deductive system', and Bion's understandings will be employed to consider the growth of Freud's thinking as he developed his successive metapsychological formulations.

Clinical theory and metapsychological theory

The apprehension of the 'selected fact' is a synthetic and creative process, one which precipitates the discovery of coherence within apparent incoherence, meaning where none had been evident. It is an activity in which cognition and emotion are intimately linked. The presence of a thinking mind, suggested Bion, depends upon the capacity to wait in uncertainty until the apprehension of a selected fact, allows meaning to become apparent. This capacity, to wait for meaning to emerge rather than to attempt to impose it, is fundamental to thinking in general, and to thinking in the clinical context in particular.

As far back as 1885 during his time in Paris at the Salpêtrière hospital with Charcot, Freud had recognized the importance of the capacity to be able to wait for, rather than attempt to impose, understanding. In his 1893 obituary tribute to Charcot, Freud described Charcot's approach: 'Here is what he himself told us about his method of working. He used to look again and again at the things that he did not understand, to deepen his impression of them day by day, till suddenly an understanding of them dawned on him' (1893 p. 12). Freud's experience with Charcot fostered the fertile line of development which would result in his description of the state of mind of the clinician conducive to the unfolding of the psychoanalytic process as one of 'evenly suspended attention' (1912 p. 111).

Bion, influenced by Freud's thinking, formulated his own prescription for the state of mind most suitable for clinical work; the analyst's participation should be one of 'negative capability', and a suspension of memory, desire and understanding (1970). Such a state of mind is conducive to the apprehension of the selected fact, linked to the process Bion designated PS → D (1963 p. 3).

The second of Bion's two forms of thinking is the rational and deductive analytic function necessary for the construction of a 'scientific deductive system'. Bion suggested that a 'scientific deductive system' can only be created when a sufficient number of 'selected fact' experiences have accumulated, and these can be worked on by conscious rational thought processes. 'Only then can the representation be formulated that will bring together the elements of coherent selected facts in a scientific deductive system' (1962 p. 73). Logical coherence and lack of contradiction are necessary conditions for any such system to be plausible.

Bion was also acutely aware of the way in which any accepted theory, or theoretical perspective, that is any existing 'coherence' or 'D' integration, will tend to 'saturate' understanding, and thus restrict perception and the ability to form new understandings. While still a medical student working in the physiology laboratory of Ernst Brücke in Vienna, Freud had likewise intuited something of this difficulty. As he wrote to his fiancé Martha:

> A failure (in research work) makes one inventive, creates a free flow of associations, brings idea after idea, whereas once success is there a certain narrow-mindedness or thick-headedness sets in so that one always keeps coming back to what has been already established and can make no new combinations. (Jones, 1953 p. 214)

In 1976 George Klein identified and differentiated two theoretical strands in Freud's thinking: a 'clinical theory' oriented towards the 'reading of intentionality' and the attribution of meaning in relation to symptoms and mental states, and a 'metapsychological theory', linked to reductionist explanatory formulations of mechanism rather than meaning (1976 p. 26). These, he believed, remained unintegrated in Freud's work.

The theoretical formulations that constitute Freud's 'clinical theory' might be described as experience near; they remain close to the kinds of understandings that emerge directly from selected fact experiences and intuitions arrived at in the clinical setting. Freud's 'metapsychological' theories on the other hand were often in the nature of imposed preconceptions, and often based on models taken from the 'natural sciences', physics and biology in particular. As Robert Caper has pointed out, there is, 'running through much of Freud's work, especially in the higher-level theorizing of what he called his "metapsychology", a wistful tendency to regard psychology as a kind of physics and to treat emotions, ideas, and states of mind in general as epiphenomenal expressions of the energic state of the mental apparatus' (1988 p. 75). As such, Freud's metapsychological formulations often remained insufficiently linked with clinical facts and experience to stand as valid inferences from observations in the psychoanalytic field. As 'scientific deductive systems' they cannot always be seen to have evolved out of accumulated 'selected fact' experiences, in the way described by Bion.

The beginnings of Freud's metapsychology: 'A kind of madness'

In 1895 Freud was working on his first attempt to formulate a coherent metapsychology; his *Project for a scientific psychology* (1895), as it has come to be known. Freud's essay was to describe and define the functioning of the mind in terms of parameters appropriate to the natural sciences; an attempt at an essentially materialist and reductionist explanation based on hypothetical mechanisms of neuronal functioning.

This quest for a neurophysiological model of the mind reflected his background in the natural sciences, and the influence of his time spent, while still a medical student, as research assistant in Brücke's physiology laboratory. As a mentor figure Brücke exercised an enormous influence upon

Freud. He was a leading scientist of the day, and one of the instigators of the 'Helmholtz' movement in biology, at the heart of which was a materialist and reductionist vision, and the belief that theories of physics and chemistry would prove sufficient to explain all human phenomena (Bernfeld, 1944 p. 348).

Freud would however soon come to see the *Project* as a failure. It is often suggested that he was unable to carry his project through because of the limited knowledge of brain function at the time, however Freud was faced with another more fundamental problem; he began to intuit that his project was impossible in its conceptual essence.

When he came to address the topic 'consciousness' Freud postulated a special category of neurons, the omega neurons, which underpinned consciousness:

> No attempt, of course, can be made to explain how it is that excitatory processes in the *w* (omega) neurones bring consciousness along with them. It is only a question of establishing a coincidence between the characteristics of consciousness that are known to us and the processes in the *w* neurones which vary in parallel with them. (1895 p. 311)

Freud's conclusion at this point was sound. In terms of explanation, 'coincidence' or correlation of the phenomena of consciousness and the phenomena of neurophysiology is the most that can be achieved. We might, however, compare this conclusion with his earlier statement of intention in his introduction to the *Project*: 'to represent psychical processes as quantitatively determinate states of specifiable material particles' (1895 p. 295). 'Represent' sounds more ambitious than correlate, and there is a sense that in the project Freud had hoped to achieve a unifying explanation of mind and brain. Consciousness lies at the heart of our conception of 'psychical processes', and if no attempt can be made to explain how neurophysiological processes bring consciousness along with them, then Freud's project was destined to end in a large measure of frustration. Attempts to explain the nature of the mind in materialist terms invariably miss the very thing, the quality of subjectivity and meaning, most distinctive in our experience of our mind. As contemporary philosopher John Searle has cogently stated, conscious mental processes possess fundamentally '*irreducible* phenomenological properties', and the need to accept this 'obvious' fact about our own experiences is as necessary as the need to accept the 'obvious facts of physics' (1998 p. 28).

Freud's relinquishing of his aspiration for a Helmholtzian explanation of the nature of the mind and subjectivity would prove difficult and painful. His letters to his friend and confidant Wilhelm Fliess speak eloquently of his struggle. On May 25, 1895, he documents his early preoccupation with his project:

> ...a man like me cannot live without a hobbyhorse, without a consuming passion, without—in Schiller's words—a tyrant. I have found one. In its service I know no limits.... During the past weeks I have devoted every free minute to such work... (Masson, 1985 p. 129)

However, some four months later Freud's letters record how his obsessive preoccupation had begun to alternate with periods of doubt, and a wish to break free of his compulsion. On October 15 he wrote: 'For two weeks I was in the throes of writing fever, believed that I had found the secret, now I know that I still haven't, and have again dropped the whole business' (ibid. p. 144).

Then on October 20:

> During an industrious night last week... the barriers suddenly lifted, the veils dropped, and everything became transparent—from the details of the neuroses to the determinants of consciousness. Everything seemed to fall into place, the cogs meshed, I had the impression that the thing now really was a machine that shortly would function on its own. The three systems of n[eurones]; the free and bound state of Qn [quantity]... [here Freud lists all the theoretical elements of his system]... finally, the factors determining consciousness, as a function of perception—all that was correct and still is today! Naturally, I can scarcely manage to contain my delight. (ibid. p. 146)

Freud's wish could not be fulfilled. Less than three weeks later, on November 8, he wrote: '... I rebelled against my tyrant. I felt overworked, irritated, confused, and incapable of mastering it all. So, I threw everything away' (ibid. p. 150). Then again on November 29: 'I no longer understand the state of mind in which I hatched the psychology...', and '... to me it appears to have been a kind of madness' (ibid. p. 152).

For all its imaginative reach, Freud's *Project* would not become the key to unlock an overarching understanding of the mind. Freud was coming to recognize he had been in the territory of 'a kind of madness', and had to mourn the loss of a delusion. This emotional reconciliation was however crucial; it would allow him to shift away from enlisting neurological mechanisms as explanatory. If his project for a scientific psychology was to succeed, it would have to become psychological in its essence. As he would state five years later, in his next great metapsychological project, *The interpretation of dreams* 'I shall remain upon psychological ground' (1900 p. 536).

If Freud was forced to mourn the failure of his *Project*, failure in his ambition to make a great discovery was inconceivable, and he proceeded to replace one project with another. I have elsewhere identified how Freud's 'seduction theory' of the origin of neuroses, took over in the wake of his abandonment of the *Project* (Schimmel, 2014 p. 122). In the letter to Fliess of October 15, 1895, in which Freud writes he has 'again dropped the whole business', he continues:

> Nevertheless, all sorts of things became clear or at least sorted themselves out. I have not lost heart. Have I revealed the great clinical secret to you, either orally or in writing?
>
> Hysteria is the consequence of a presexual *sexual shock*. (Masson, 1985 p. 144)

Impressed by his patients accounts of apparent childhood sexual 'shocks', Freud came to the conclusion that the experiences they recounted were causally necessary for the genesis of hysterical neuroses. In April 1896 Freud would expound this theory in 'The etiology of hysteria', a paper read to the Society for Psychiatry and Neurology in Vienna. Writing to Fliess he claimed his lecture, 'was given an icy reception by the asses.... And this, after one has demonstrated to them the solution of a more-than-one-thousand-year-old problem, a *caput nili* (source of the Nile)! They can go to hell, euphemistically expressed' (ibid. p. 184).

Mourning and self-analysis

Freud was in 'conquistador' mode (Schimmel, 2014), and in place of his grand explanatory metapsychology, he now proposed a grand explanatory theory based, he believed, directly upon clinical experience. However, his seduction hypothesis would, in turn, prove more fantasy than reality; in Bion's terms, not a true 'selected fact' discovered in clinical experience, but rather a premature and delusional synthesis imposed on that experience. The seduction hypothesis would, of necessity, be abandoned in its turn.

In 1897 Freud wrote to Fliess with seeming equanimity: 'And now I want to confide in you immediately the great secret that has been slowly dawning on me in the last few months. I no longer believe in my *neurotica*' (Masson, 1985 p. 264). 'Neurotica' refers to Freud's seduction theory of the neuroses. Towards the end of this same letter he adds:

> In this collapse of everything valuable, the psychological alone has remained untouched. The dream (book) stands entirely secure and my beginnings of the metapsychological work have only grown in my estimation. It is a pity that one cannot make a living, for instance, on dream interpretation! (ibid. p. 266)

We might wonder if again Freud was only able to relinquish his grand theory of the etiology of the neuroses when he was advanced enough with a replacement project; one that would result in *The interpretation of dreams* (1900). The situation was however complex. Freud's letting go of his 'neurotica' was one outcome of the long and painful process of mourning following the death of his father, and a consequence of the experience that has come to be known as his 'self-analysis'.

The beginning of Freud's self-analysis can be dated, somewhat arbitrarily, to his 'dream of Irma's injection' in July 1895, and his attempted analysis of this 'specimen dream' as recorded in chapter II of *The interpretation of dreams*. With his own dreams, as with his patients', he would employ his technique of 'free-association'. When, in October 1986 Freud's father died, his experience of mourning shifted the process of self-analysis from a somewhat intellectual one of dream analysis, into a lived emotional imperative. As Anzieu has commented: 'Mourning set in motion a process of intense psychical work in Freud' (1986 p. 175).

As Freud came to recognize, *The interpretation of dreams* was born of his self-analysis. In the 1908 preface to the second edition he wrote:

> For this book has a further subjective significance for me personally—a significance which I only grasped after I had completed it. It was, I found, a portion of my own self-analysis, my reaction to my father's death—that is to say, to the most important event, the most poignant loss, of a man's life. (1900 p. xxvi)

Years later he would write to Ernest Jones that the death of his father 'revolutioned my soul' (Gay, 1988 p. 390).

In *Studies on hysteria* (1895), Freud's first comprehensive account of his developing clinical thinking and theory, he had attempted to 'look again and again at the things that he did not understand' (1893 p. 12), in order to derive working hypotheses directly from experience with patients. With *The interpretation of dreams* he was returning to clinical exploration, only this time adding his own dreams as part of his resource of 'clinical' material. Then, in chapter VII of his 'dream book', he proposed the new metapsychological formulations that have come to be known as his 'topographical model'. Having adopted a purely psychological vertex, and using the new clinical insights arising from his work on dreams, Freud reformulated his metapsychological thinking into the new topographical model, while at the same time retaining many elements of the mechanistic vision of the *Project*. His 'wistful tendency to regard psychology as a kind of physics' (Caper, 1988 p. 75) would always linger.

Despite the inevitable limitations of any attempt at 'self-analysis', Freud's experience of mourning had created an intense inward focus, and his technique of free association was conducive to the discovery of unexpected coherence and new meanings through the 'selected fact' experience. In 1894, prior to his self-analysis, Freud had been experiencing episodes of quite debilitating somatic symptoms, alongside apparently melancholic symptoms (Masson, 1985 p. 67). Anzieu (1986 p. 561) has observed that the self-analysis does appear to have had a transformative effect upon Freud's melancholic disposition. The period of self-analysis and the writing of his 'dream book' is arguably the most creative of his life. Freud's mourning stimulated a reappraisal of his relationship with his father, and he discovered within himself evidence of a deep ambivalence. As Anzieu writes: 'For the first time, the parricidal dimension of the Oedipal organization is foreshadowed' (1986 p. 172). All of this would contribute in turn to his abandonment of the seduction hypothesis.

Freud had previously come to regard several of his siblings as afflicted with hysteria, and in order to line his 'diagnostic' conclusions up with his seduction hypothesis had been forced to the further conclusion that his own father was somehow responsible. On February 8, 1897, he wrote to Fliess: 'Unfortunately, my own father was one of these perverts and is responsible for the hysteria of my brother (all of whose symptoms are identifications) and those of several younger sisters' (Masson, 1985 p. 230). As his self-analysis progressed, this construction began to look increasingly implausible. Among the reasons for abandoning the seduction theory, outlined in his famous letter to Fliess of September 21, 1897, was the necessity '...that in all cases, the *father*, not excluding my own, had to be accused of being perverse... whereas surely such widespread perversions against children are not very probable' (Masson, 1985 p. 264). Freud was beginning to take responsibility for his 'unconscious phantasies' and what he had referred to as 'My little hysteria' (ibid. p. 261).

A further reason, offered in the letter of September 21, for abandoning his seduction hypothesis was, 'the certain insight that there are no indications of reality in the unconscious, so that one cannot distinguish between truth and fiction that has been cathected with affect' (ibid. p. 264). Freud was abandoning another mechanistic model, one locating the causes of specific neuroses in specific sorts of developmental experiences. He was beginning to understand how the human mind is active in creating meaning out of the circumstances of its own experience. If we were searching for a point in Freud's life where he might have been said to have discovered psychoanalysis, this is perhaps the best candidate. Janet Malcolm has written: 'traditional accounts of the emergence of psychoanalysis all agree that Freud's realization that his theory was wrong was the fulcrum of his momentous discovery of the cornerstones of psychoanalytic theory: infantile sexuality and the Oedipus complex' (Malcolm, 1984 p. 21). However, more fundamental to psychoanalysis than infantile sexuality or the Oedipus complex, was the realization: 'there are no indications of reality in the unconscious.' Freud was recognizing the creative agency in the activity of the mind and beginning to recognize the nature of an alternative reality, that of unconscious phantasy; both his clinical thinking and metapsychological formulations would be altered accordingly.

Freud's self-analysis took place within a complex web of relationships and events, including his relationship with Wilhelm Fliess and the notorious Emma Eckstein affair. Fliess, an ENT surgeon, had operated at Freud's request upon the nose of one of Freud's patient's, Emma Eckstein, in 1895. The results were catastrophic with Eckstein suffering repeated life threatening hemorrhages as a result of Fliess's poor surgical practice. Although it would take Freud years to fully acknowledge the impact of these events, his confidence in Fliess was shattered, and he would gradually distance himself from his confidant.

One after another of Freud's cherished certainties, points of view, theories, and relationships were being challenged, reassessed, and often found wanting. Alongside the loss of his father Freud was questioning old assumptions. In October 1897, not long after the abandonment of his seduction hypothesis, Freud wrote to Fliess, 'I live only of the "inner work"', and:

> Many a sad secret of life is here followed back to its first roots; many a pride and privilege are made aware of their humble origins. All of what I experienced with my patients, as a third (person) I find again here—days when I drag myself about dejected because I have understood nothing of the dream, of the fantasy, of the mood of the day; and then again days when a flash of lightening illuminates the interrelations and lets me understand the past as a preparation for the present. (Masson, 1985 p. 274)

Contrast the tone and emphasis here, to that of Freud's letter two years earlier, at the peak of his enthusiasm for his *Project*:

> ...the barriers suddenly lifted, the veils dropped, and everything became transparent.... Everything seemed to fall into place, the cogs meshed, I had the impression that the thing now really was a machine that shortly would function on its own. (ibid p. 146)

The shift is from manic defence to mourning, and Freud was learning to live with greater uncertainty. In the course of these upheavals, Freud the thinker was gaining in strength and the 'dream book' was taking shape within his mind. Using his clinical experience to date, his developing understanding of dreams, and conceptual elements salvaged from the *Project*, Freud began constructing the topographical metapsychological framework of *The interpretation of dreams*. While the mechanistic elements of this framework would eventually prove limiting, it was one he could build on.

The disillusionment of the First World War

At the outbreak of World War I in 1914, Freud, aged 58, was firmly on the side of the Austro-Hungarian alliance. On the declaration of war, wrote Ernest Jones, Freud 'was quite carried away, could not think of any work, and spent his time discussing the events of the day with his brother Alexander. As he put it: "All my libido is given to Austro-Hungary"' (Jones, 1955 p. 192).

In Peter Gay's words, Freud 'indulged himself in partisan credulity' (1988 p. 349), and was initially optimistic about a relatively short war and a German victory. More significantly, he evinced a surprisingly naïve attitude as to the likely consequences of the conflict. Warfare would, he believed or imagined, be conducted in a civilized manner; as 'a chivalrous passage of arms', as he put it in his 1915 essay 'The disillusionment of war' (1915d p. 278).

Freud's enthusiasm subsided as the realities of the war began to become clear, and the conflict came closer to home when the eldest of his three sons, Martin, enrolled in August 1914. As his letters to Lou Andreas-Salomé (Pfeiffer, 1963), and Karl Abraham (Abraham H C and Freud E L, 1965) suggest, in response to his experience of the war he entered a circumscribed episode of depression in the latter part of 1914. Characteristically, Freud would be able to transform this circumscribed melancholia into an experience of mourning, and this process is, I believe, recorded in three essays: 'The disillusionment of war', and 'Our attitude towards death', both written in early in 1915 and published together (1915d); and 'On transience', written in November 1915, and published in 1916.

In 'The disillusionment of war', Freud attempted to come to terms with the stark reality of the carnage resulting from the attempted military solution. He acknowledges that he had been under the sway of an illusion, but 'the war in which we had refused to believe broke out, and it brought—

disillusionment' (1915d p. 278). Freud had not anticipated the extent of mankind's capacity for aggression and destruction.

In November 1914, as the reality of war hit home, he wrote to Lou Andreas-Salomé:

> I do not doubt that mankind will survive even this war, but I know for certain that for me and my contemporaries the world will never again be a happy place. It is too hideous. And the saddest thing about it is that it is exactly the way we should have expected people to behave from our knowledge of psycho-analysis. (Pfeiffer, 1963 p. 21)

If, from his knowledge of psychoanalysis, Freud 'should have expected' people to behave in this way, the fact is he did not. In 'The disillusionment of war' he goes on to reflect that bearing the pain of disillusionment allows greater contact with reality:

> We welcome illusions because they spare us unpleasurable feelings and enable us to enjoy satisfactions instead. We must not complain, then, if now and again they come into collision with some portion of reality and are shattered against it. (1915d p. 280)

In 'Our attitude towards death' (1915d), Freud develops a related theme, that the recognition and acceptance of the reality of death allows life to become fuller and more complete.

Then in November 1915, Freud wrote his famous short essay 'On transience' (1916). In this essay, Freud recalls a walk in the countryside with a 'taciturn friend' and a 'young but already famous poet' which took place before the outbreak of the war. The poet expressed the view that because all beauty in the world was transient and 'fated to extinction' (1916

p. 305), there could be no joy in the beauty of nature, or in the works of man. Freud counters the poet's pessimistic view that this transience entails any loss of worth. He asserts, 'A flower that blossoms only for a single night does not seem to us on that account less lovely', but these considerations seemed to make little impression either upon the poet or Freud's friend. Freud concludes, 'some powerful emotional factor was at work which was disturbing their judgment, and I believed later that I had discovered what it was. What spoilt their enjoyment of beauty must have been a revolt in their minds against mourning' (1916 p. 306).

Freud speculates that to invest 'libido' in an object, in other words to 'love', entails the risk of loss and potential pain, and anticipating this, 'the mind instinctively recoils from anything that is painful' (1916 p. 306). He suggests that the young poet's melancholic disposition arises out of an aversion to psychic pain. In the face of an inability to mourn, the reality of transience leads to despondency.

Perhaps 'On transience' might be read as a kind of psychoanalytic allegory of internal objects and the centrality of mourning (Schimmel, 2014). There are two 'before the war' figures: Freud, who the text suggests possesses the capacity to mourn, and the poet, who has not realized such a capacity. Might not both represent aspects of Freud himself? Then the 'war broke out and robbed the world of its beauties', thus initiating a process of mourning, but 'once the mourning is over, it will be found that our high opinion of the riches of civilization has lost nothing from our discovery of their fragility. We shall build up again all that the war has destroyed, and perhaps on firmer ground and more lastingly than before' (1916 p. 307). An experience of loss is necessary to initiate a mourning, which may in turn increase the emotional capacity of the mind, potentially transforming the 'melancholic' part of the mind into one more capable of mourning. Thus, the mind will find itself 'on firmer ground and more lastingly than before.'

In this essay we sense Freud feels his own libido is, after a period of mourning, 'once more free' (1916 p. 307); freed, we might infer, from attachment to illusory ideals such as the 'lofty impartiality of our science' (1916 p. 307), and the idealized state of mind he described in 'The disillusionment of war'.

At the beginning of 'Mourning and melancholia' Freud identifies 'the exciting causes' of mourning as, 'the reaction to the loss of a loved person, or to the loss of some abstraction which has taken the place of one, such as one's country, liberty, an ideal, and so on' (1917 p. 243). Freud was mourning the loss of an ideal, his own somewhat idealized world view, and this process of mourning appears to have led to a transformation of his initial melancholic reaction to the reality of the war: 'the world will never again be a happy place' (Pfeiffer, 1963 p. 21). The proposed reading of 'On transience' would also suggest that this process of working through exerted a further transformative and lasting effect upon Freud's 'melancholic' disposition.

'The disillusionment of the war' was written more or less concurrently with 'Mourning and melancholia', and it would seem probable that Freud's experience of disillusion, despondency and mourning, contributed in turn to the precipitation of a number of his existing conceptual formulations and clinical intuitions into his new understanding of the nature of mourning and melancholia.

Mourning and melancholia: Freud's alternative metapsychology

In 'On narcissism', completed early in 1914, Freud reflected that theoretical constructions 'are not the foundation of science, upon which everything rests: that foundation is observation alone. They are not the bottom but the top of the whole structure, and they can be replaced or discarded without damaging it' (1914 p. 77). George Makari suggests that in writing these words, Freud 'simply could not be taken seriously' (2008 p. 299). Makari observes that Freud's dogmatic insistence on acceptance of his theoretical construction of psychosexuality as the fundamental organizing principle of the mind, had led to a situation where, 'Matters of close clinical observation and inference had become secondary to verifying the sexual unconscious wherever it could be found' (2008 p. 298).

However, in 'Mourning and melancholia', a year after his comment that the foundation of science is observation alone, Freud apparently takes his own injunction to heart, returning to 'first principles' in order to try and look afresh at the observable clinical facts of melancholia in relation to mourning. It is this decision to remain close to clinical experience, to try to construct understanding from the ground up, that allows the emergence of new elements of theory.

Freud begins his essay with the recognition of the clinical similarities between states of mourning and states of melancholia, but notes one crucial difference. Melancholic states manifest the presence of a hatred within the mind, that appears to be turned upon the sufferer's own self. The recognition of this hostile disposition towards the self in melancholia, but not in mourning, functions in his text as a 'selected fact', which creates coherence within the picture of melancholia, and is employed to suggest remarkable new insights.

Freud speculates that the melancholic's attitude of hostility towards a part of his own ego is an aggressive force which has been turned back upon the self, as a result of identification with a lost or disappointing 'object':

> If the love for the object—a love which cannot be given up though the object itself is given up—takes refuge in narcissistic identification, then the hate comes into operation on this substitutive object, abusing it, debasing it, making it suffer and deriving sadistic satisfaction from its suffering. (1917 p. 251)

This conception, as presented in 'Mourning and melancholia', of a dynamic relationship, potentially co-operative or antagonistic, between different aspects of the mind, due to the internalization of what Freud termed an 'object-relationship' (1917 p. 249), would prove transformative.

From a metapsychological vertex Freud's essay represented a new synthesis. I will identify three important 'metapsychological' shifts. Most fundamental and important was Freud's new object relational perspective, which took him beyond his existing theory. In 'Mourning and melancholia' Freud is conceptualizing the development of the mind less in terms of the vicissitudes of abstracted forces of differing drives or instincts, and more in terms of the vicissitudes of previous relationships, in particular experiences of disappointment and loss. While Freud makes frequent reference to his psychosexual conceptual framework of libido and cathexis, he also allows himself the freedom to think beyond it, and his analysis moves towards consideration of forces couched more directly in emotional terms; love and hate as opposing currents within the mind and the capacity to mourn come to the fore. For example, having written of a 'threatened libidinal cathexis at length abandoning the object', his language shifts, becoming more imaginatively and emotionally evocative, and in so doing, startles: 'So by taking flight into the ego love escapes extinction' (1917 p. 257). Freud's perspective becomes more 'relational' as he introduces the idea of the quality of the experience of relationship with the 'object' as giving shape to the internal world. This leads to a more complex conception of internal objects, along with the idea of the internalization of aspects of an 'object-relationship', resulting in a conception of alive relationships and potential conflicts between these 'objects' in the inner world, or as we would say between parts of the mind. Linked to this is the importance of ambivalence, which is becoming central to Freud's understanding (Ogden, 2005).

Freud was not, of course, repudiating his drive/instinct metapsychology, and the second shift identified occurs within that framework. It is a shift of emphasis, with aggressive and hostile forces being given greater recognition. Freud had always been reluctant to assign primacy to aggressive and destructive forces within the mind. In his 'Little Hans' case history of 1909, he wrote: 'I cannot bring myself to assume the existence of a special aggressive instinct alongside of the familiar instincts of self-preservation and of sex, and on an equal footing with them' (1909 p. 140).

Freud had long been trying to think about the place of the forces of aggression and destructiveness within the mind, and his reluctance to assign them greater importance would seem, as much as anything, to have been a consequence of his wish to maintain the illusions he would come to acknowledge in 'The disillusionment of war'. Confronted with the stark reality of the war he felt compelled, it seems, to redress the imbalance. In 'Mourning and melancholia' aggressive and hostile forces are recognized more in their own right, and greater autonomy is attributed to them. At this stage, however, Freud does not elevate them to the level of a primary drive as he would later do in 'Beyond the pleasure principle' (1920). They remain conceptualized as secondary, arising presumably from frustrations of the libido and disappointments to the ego.

A third fundamental shift implicit in 'Mourning and melancholia' is the suggestion that development of the capacity to mourn is central to the development of the mind. Freud suggests that a melancholic state of mind is the manifestation of a narcissistic disturbance, linked to an inability to mourn, and this has come about, he implies, as a consequence of a previous identification with a disappointing, ambivalently regarded, and abandoned object. A 'narcissistic identification with the object then becomes a substitute for the erotic cathexis' (1917 p. 249). Although it is not made explicit, Freud seems to suggest that developmentally there has been an 'erotic' disappointment, and melancholia represents the consequence of an attempt to evade the trauma or psychic pain of this loss. An inability to mourn is therefore a consequence of a previous failure to mourn.

This consideration of the capacity to mourn as a fundamental achievement of the mind links with Freud's shift towards addressing questions of emotional meaning much more directly and in their own terms. Mourning is conceptualized in terms of loss, pain, relationships and meaning. The vicissitudes of relationships and the resulting 'identifications' and emotional dispositions are now in the foreground.

When, in 1897, Freud abandoned his 'seduction hypothesis', he concluded the unconscious does not simply retain some kind of faithful record of actual events; 'there are no indications of reality in the unconscious', as he wrote to Fliess (Masson, 1985 p. 264). As suggested, this position involved recognition that the mind is active in creating meaning out of the circumstances of its experience. If, as Freud seems to suggest in 'Mourning and melancholia', and makes explicit in 'On transience', an inability to mourn represents an attempt to evade the psychic pain of loss, then a new dimension is potentially added to the concept of agency within the mind. The inherent capacity of the mind to tolerate psychic pain becomes a determining factor shaping emotional growth, and a condition for maintaining contact with psychic reality.

Freud is adding a further dimension to his distinction between pleasure principle and reality principle, as outlined in 'Formulations on the two principles of mental functioning'. The formulations in this short 1911 paper retain the mechanistic quality that characterizes most of Freud's metapsychological writing. Reality is a potential source of 'unpleasure', while the capacity to tolerate such unpleasure can strengthen the development of the 'impartial passing of judgement' (1911 p. 221) in relation to reality; the 'reality principle'. But ultimately, suggests Freud, this orientation towards reality remains in the service of the pleasure principle: 'the substitution of the reality principle for the pleasure principle implies no deposing of the pleasure principle, but only a safeguarding of it' (1911 p. 223).

However, implicitly in 'Mourning and melancholia', and explicitly in 'On transience', the capacity to tolerate the psychic pain of loss is understood to facilitate the development of a capacity to mourn. In 'On transience' development of the capacity to mourn is understood in turn to preserve hope, and so further increases the capacity to tolerate disappointment, loss, and emotional pain, and facilitates the growth of the mind. These new formulations suggest a position where contact with reality, even if painful, is judged, not just as a form of enlightened self-interest and a transformation of the pleasure principle, but rather as an emotional preference. Despite the potential pain involved, contact with reality is *felt* to be preferable; whether it leads to 'pleasure' or 'unpleasure' becomes secondary. Paradoxically, at least in terms of Freud's 'two principles' model, 'On transience' suggests that the domination of the pleasure principle might actually compromise the mind, not just in its function as an arbiter of reality, but in its emotional capacity; it is the figure of the poet who in the attempt to avoid pain is condemned to melancholia and so unable to experience pleasure in the world.

Consideration of how difficult, or impossible, it is to reconcile the painful nature of the experience of mourning with Freud's idea of the 'pleasure principle' as the fundamental organizing principle of the human mind, leads to the realization of just how far reaching was Freud's shift in suggesting the capacity to mourn was the central achievement of the human mind. In 'Mourning and melancholia' for the first time Freud steps 'beyond the pleasure principle', and far more convincingly than he will later do in his text of that name.

George Makari has commented that in response to the horrors of the war, Freud the thinker had overthrown Freud the defender of his own orthodoxy of the centrality of psycho-sexuality. As Makari suggests, Freud's shift to the new theory of life and death instincts in 'Beyond the pleasure principle' was a 'staggering about face' (2008 p. 319). Nevertheless this 'about face' remained entirely within the orthodoxy of his metapsychology of instinct theory. In 'Mourning and melancholia', Freud the thinker more or less sidesteps his instinct theory to formulate an essentially new conceptual framework. If this did not seem such a dramatic and contentious shift as that of 'Beyond the pleasure principle', in reality it would prove the more radical one.

A synthesis of clinical thinking and metapsychological theory

As noted, Freud's predilection for the mechanistic metapsychological formulations of his 1895 *Project* would remain throughout his life. In 'The unconscious', one of the 1915 'metapsychological papers', he defined his metapsychology as having topographical, economic, and dynamic dimensions. The term 'topographical' carries the inference of the dimensionality of physical space; 'economic' carries the emphasis on quantity as a factor in explanation, while 'dynamic' also resonates with the idea of dynamic forces in physics. Together the three dimensions reflect Freud's on-going wish to formulate theories that include explanatory parameters compatible with those employed in the natural sciences.

George Klein has emphasized that Freud's clinical theory of meaning, and his metapsychological theory of mechanisms, are 'two lines of development (that) express different conceptions of what psychoanalysis is and ought to be' (1976 p. 25). However, 'the two orientations have often been confounded…' (1976 p. 26). The essence of psychoanalytic explanation, suggested Klein, is clinical explanation, beginning from an understanding of the subject's own vantage point; without the exploration of subjectivity explanation is not possible. He viewed Freud's metapsychological explanations of mechanism as a distraction, because they are not inherent in the kind of explanation psychoanalysis can generate.

Klein was one of a number of commentators in North America, who, from the 1960s through to the 1980s, concluded that the metapsychological project that was Freudian 'ego psychology' had proved a dead end (Holt, 1985; Hale, 1995). Klein further concluded that the metapsychological project was in itself untenable and that valid psychoanalytic theory needed to remain clinical theory. Despite something of a consensus that the mechanistic elements of Freud's metapsychology and ego-psychology had become a cul-de-sac, not all agreed that abandoning these elements need necessarily entail abandoning the metapsychological project in its entirety (Holt, 1985). A further difficulty was that within the 'metapsychological' and 'clinical' theory dichotomy, both elude clear differentiation and definition, because when theories are scrutinized there is great difficulty in defining a boundary between one kind of theory and another (ibid. 1985).

'Mourning and melancholia' offers a challenge to George Klein's contention that Freud was never able to satisfactorily resolve the dichotomy that existed between his metapsychology and his clinical theory of meaning and intentionality. Once again 'Mourning and melancholia' stands alone, because in this essay I think Freud does meet with substantial success in bridging the gap between clinical phenomena and explanation, and metapsychological formulations at a higher level of abstraction; that is in showing how higher-level theoretical formulations might be derived from clinical observation and experience.

As noted, Freud's starting point is his description of the characteristic features of melancholia and mourning. These are presented as generalized pictures representing the typical person in mourning, and the typical melancholic patient:

> The distinguishing mental features of melancholia are a profoundly painful dejection, cessation of interest in the outside world, loss of the capacity to love, inhibition of all activity, and a lowering

> of the self-regarding feelings to a degree that finds utterances in self-reproaches and self-revilings, and culminates in a delusional expectation of punishment. (1917 p. 244)

Freud writes with clarity and authority, not the arbitrary authority of the Freud the dogmatist, but the authority of Freud the thinker, one grounded in clinical experience and accumulated knowledge. Throughout the text Freud continues to reference back to clinical observation and inference. For example:

> If one listens patiently to a melancholic's many and various self-accusations, one cannot in the end avoid the impression that the most violent of them are hardly at all applicable to the patient himself, but with some insignificant modifications they do fit someone else, someone whom the patient loves or has loved or should love. (1917 p. 248)

Despite the overt and apparent self-accusations and attack, there are suggestions and indications of latent accusations against another. Freud intuits that the melancholic's behaviour proceeds from 'a mental constellation of revolt, which has then, by a certain process, passed over into the crushed state of melancholia' (1917 p. 248). He then infers that there must have once been an object-relationship that was 'shattered', along with the psychic consequences of this. Gradually, relentlessly almost, Freud builds up his object-relational perspective and theory. As Ogden observes, 'Freud, for the first time, is gathering together into a coherent narrative expressed in higher order theoretical terms his newly conceived revised model of the mind' (2005 p. 33).

Beginning with his generalized observational data, Freud infers emotional meanings and psychic intentions. These elements of clinical theory arise by direct inference from observation, and from these accumulated inferences he abstracts in turn the beginning elements of his new theoretical formulation. There is an evolution from clinical facts towards metapsychological understanding, and a new synthesis appears to be achieved.

As suggested, Freud does not abandon his existing metapsychological perspective, but he is able to stand aside from this in order to arrive at his new formulations. For example, having identified 'economics' as one of the three legs of his existing metapsychology in 'The unconscious' (1915c), now in 'Mourning and melancholia' Freud considers the slow process of emotional working through that is characteristic of successful mourning, and comments, 'Why this ... should be so extraordinarily painful is not at all easy to explain in terms of economics' (1917 p. 245). An 'economic' factor is clearly in evidence, but as Freud acknowledges, the recognition of this doesn't seem to offer explanatory help in trying to understand the psychic pain involved, or its emotional meaning for the sufferer.

'Mourning and melancholia' conveys a sense of careful observation of the field until understanding dawned. Although we cannot know exactly how Freud came to his formulations, as Ogden observes, the impression the text creates upon the reader is of Freud doing his thinking in the very act of writing (2005 p. 27). The idea of the 'selected fact' experience is particularly relevant, because reading the text conveys the sense of coherence being discovered in the field of observation; a discovery that the reader can potentially experience for him or herself in the very act of reading.

Throughout 'Mourning and melancholia' Freud's formulations remain linked to his scientific 'foundation' of observation (1914 p. 77). Part of the impact of the text would seem accounted for by the synthesis Freud was able to achieve between his clinical observation and interpretation, and his metapsychological construction of theory, along with the experience of coherence that this offers the reader.

Turning to the general problem raised by George Klein of the relation of 'clinical theory' and 'metapsychological theory', perhaps this might be reframed through consideration of Bion's distinction between the integrative thinking of the 'selected fact' experience, and the rational and logical thinking, necessary for the construction of a theoretical system. According to Bion's formulation, a valid 'scientific deductive system' in any scientific endeavour is constructed out of an accumulation of selected fact experiences. To the extent psychoanalysis is a scientific endeavour, a psychoanalytic theory must find its origins in the accumulation of psychoanalytic experience and evidence, and the origin of any theory must be able to be traced to clinical facts and their interpretation. Within this frame the distinction between 'clinical theory' and 'metapsychological theory' would seem to resolve into a continuum of theory at differing levels of abstraction; the greater the level of abstraction the more 'metapsychological' the theory. This perspective is, of course, essentially that of the vertical axis of Bion's grid. Accumulated 'conceptions' (row E), potentially evolve into 'concepts' (row F), and from accumulated concepts a 'scientific deductive system' (row G), may eventually be formulated.

Bion (1970) advocated the frame of mind appropriate to the clinical encounter as one which eschews memory, desire and understanding; one of 'negative capability'. In the theoretical conceptual field, as in the clinical, existing conceptions and concepts may limit the extent to which new conceptual coherence and understanding may be discovered. The growth or evolution of theoretical understanding therefore, is also potentially facilitated by such a frame of mind. Conceptions formed at one level of abstraction, one row of the grid, may function in a pre-conceptive capacity for the formulation of conceptions at the next level, until a 'scientific deductive system' can be formulated. Then, once formulated, such a system must be subject to, and accord with, the laws of logic. Like George Klein, Bion believed that psychoanalytic theory must remain, in essence, clinical, but unlike Klein, Bion viewed the formulation of psychoanalytic theory at higher levels of abstraction as a valid conceptual project.

Following Bion's understandings of how thinking develops, the distinction between 'clinical' theory and 'metapsychological' theory might be resolved into a distinction between clinical understanding, that is the understanding specific to a particular clinical experience, and psychoanalytic theory, that is any attempt to generalize from accumulated clinical experience. Psychoanalytic theories are then formulated at different levels of abstraction.

Within this frame all theory must find its origin within the subjective experiences of the clinical encounter, but it would also seem inevitable that the subjectivity that has contributed to clinical experience and understanding will be lost in the construction of a theory that incorporates that understanding. Furthermore, it would seem inevitable that theoretical models designed to explicate theories at higher levels of abstraction, are likely to incorporate mechanized and concretized elements representational of hypothetical psychic functions. The concept of an 'internal object' would seem to offer an example of such a representation. The hypothetical process of internalization of an external 'object', that is an aspect of a person or some element of personality, and the transformation of this into some form of internal personality function, is 'objectified' in the very term.

Freud's journey of mourning

We might expect the question of the nature of melancholia to have been of vital importance for Freud, as there is evidence that throughout his life, he was subject to episodes that might be considered melancholic or had at least an identifiable melancholic dimension. The most sustained and important of these was in the years preceding and leading into his self-analysis (Schimmel, 2014 p. 113). He would not seem to have experienced such 'melancholic' intensity subsequently.

From the beginning of Freud's self-analysis an emotional process of reappraisal and the questioning of certainties was set in train. Beginning with relinquishing his grand hopes for his 1895 *Project*, and subsequently his replacement 'seduction theory', the shifts and developments in his theory were intimately linked to his own emotional journey. Freud's experience of mourning following the death of his father was profound, deepening the self-analysis, and greatly expanding his mind. As he wrote, it 'revolutioned my soul' (Gay, 1988 p. 390).

Freud would undergo a further period of despondency, depression, and mourning, following the outbreak of the First World War. Again, he was acutely aware of the impact of this experience; as he acknowledged, his belief in mankind's capacity to rise above aggression and destructiveness was 'shattered' (1915d p. 280). Freud's formulations of the process of mourning as potentially transformative in 'Mourning and melancholia' and 'On transience', surely had their origin in his own transformational experiences of mourning. We can imagine that the unsettling of his existing world view, his loss of 'illusions' in 1914 and 1915, would have resonated with the experience of his self-analysis, so that his awareness of the centrality of mourning in psychic growth was sharpened.

In 1914 Freud was again looking more deeply into his own experience for insight and understanding. Just as he had drawn on his own dreams in writing *The interpretation of dreams*, his experiences both of melancholia and mourning seem to have become essential 'clinical material' for the writing of 'Mourning and melancholia'; Freud's essay appears to have been the outcome of a further piece of self-analytic work. Perhaps there is a significant conjunction in his reference to the explanatory value of dreams in the opening sentence of 'Mourning and melancholia':

> Dreams having served us as the prototype in normal life of narcissistic mental disorders, we will now try to throw some light on the nature of melancholia by comparing it with the normal affect of mourning. (1917 p. 243)

Ernest Jones (1955 p. 368) claimed that Freud had expounded the central idea of 'Mourning and melancholia' to him as early as January, 1914. Freud had certainly been thinking about the elements of the theory that would cohere in 'Mourning and melancholia' for some time. Again, a link can be traced as far back as his self-analysis when he wrote to Fliess in 1897, suggesting that it is a 'manifestation of mourning' for the parents, 'to reproach oneself for their death (so-called melancholia)', because of repressed 'hostile impulses' towards them (Masson, 1985 p. 250).

Freud appears to have drawn substantially on Abraham's thinking, as for example, Abraham's 1911 conclusion, that in melancholic states, 'it could be discovered that the disease proceeded from an attitude of hate which was paralyzing the patient's capacity to love' (1911 p. 143), and also Abraham's emphasis of the link between melancholia and the oral stage (Strachey, 1957 p. 239).

A letter to Ferenczi in 1912 perhaps hints at Freud's otherwise unacknowledged insecurities about his existing formulations. Freud writes of his broken relationship with Jung and his insistence on the centrality of psychosexuality, 'Must I always be right, always be the better one? In the long run it becomes downright improbably to one' (Brabant et al, 1992 p. 340). While Freud would not give any ground in the battle with Jung, as Makari observes there is 'a note of sadness and uncharacteristic self-doubt' (Makari, 2008 p. 288). Anzieu (1986 p. 210) has suggested that the break with Jung initiated a process of mourning that may have contributed to the writing of 'Mourning and melancholia', as may have the death of Freud's half-brother Emanuel in 1914.

In 1913, with the writing of *Totem and taboo*, Freud speculated about the way social institutions fulfilled the need to suppress the collective manifestations of human ambivalence and potential aggression. In terms of economics, Freud's focus in *Totem and taboo* seemed to shift from the centrality of psychosexuality towards consideration of the fate of aggressive forces within the mind (Freud, 1913). Then, in 1914, Freud published his theory of narcissism, constructing an essential part of the theoretical framework necessary for the conceptualization of the origins of melancholia (Ogden, 2005 p. 35).

In the latter part of 1914, these elements of thinking and theory that Freud had been considering for some time, appear to have precipitated out into a new coherence. While we cannot know quite how this came about, it is the hypothesis of this paper that Freud's personal journey of mourning was transformative, and that, in the realm of his 'metapsychology', 'Mourning and melancholia' was the outcome.

The centrality of mourning, that is the capacity to tolerate the psychic pain of loss, as a condition for maintaining contact with psychic reality, is a clinical fact. It is as if, for Freud, the evidence for the centrality of this clinical fact was gradually building until in 'Mourning and melancholia' it became the central and 'selected' fact.

Concluding comments

To the extent psychoanalysis possesses a shared metapsychology in the midst of contemporary theoretical diversity, this might be broadly delineated as an 'object relations' metapsychology. The essential elements of contemporary object relations thinking were already present in Freud's 1915 formulations, including the concept of the process he called 'identification' whereby aspects of an 'object' or 'object relationship' are internalized, influence the function of the mind, and confer meaning upon experience.

In 1915 Freud put forward a coherent, integrating, and I think convincing, theoretical model of the nature of melancholic depression, as well as a sketch outline of a new model of the mind, also in sufficient detail to be convincing. In coming to his new formulations it would appear that Freud did not acknowledge the full extent of his debt to Abraham. However, it was Freud who was able to bring a number of clinical facts and lines of theoretical development into coherence, and in so doing open a new conceptual door. Through this door psychoanalysis would eventually take a decisive step.

I have suggested that it became possible for Freud to write 'Mourning and melancholia' because it was written out of his transformative experiences of mourning. These experiences appear to have been fundamental in fostering a process of emotional growth that would eventually allow him to begin to move beyond the reductionist models of the mind which dominated so much of his conceptual thinking. This shift was in evidence in *The interpretation of dreams*, but would only find its full expression fifteen years later in 'Mourning and melancholia'.

As noted, Freud famously suggested that insights such as contained in *The interpretation of dreams*, could be expected but once in a lifetime. Yet for all the brilliance of his dream book, some of Freud's central theses have not stood the test of time. In 'Mourning and melancholia' Freud captured fundamental understandings about the origin of melancholic states and about the growth of the human mind, which being accurate enough, have stood that test. Freud's essay represented the culmination of a process of personal transformation and of a line of inquiry that had been gradually evolving. It is packed with insights and achieves an extraordinary economy of expression. For these reasons, despite its brevity, 'Mourning and melancholia' is, I believe, the psychoanalytic text in which Freud's genius found its fullest expression.

References

Abraham, H.C. & Freud, E.L. (Eds.) (1965). *The Letters of Sigmund Freud and Karl Abraham 1907–1926.* New York: Basic Books.

Abraham, K. (1979). *Karl Abraham: Selected Papers on Psychoanalysis* (pp. 137–156). London: Karnac. (Original work published 1911).

Anzieu, D. (1986). *Freud's self-analysis.* London: The Hogarth Press and the Institute of Psycho-analysis.

Bernfeld, S. (1944). Freud's earliest theories and the school of Helmholtz. *Psychoanalytic Quarterly* 13:341–362

Bion, W.R. (1998). *Learning from Experience.* Northvale, New Jersey: Jason Aronson. (Original work published 1962).

——— (1963). *Elements of Psychoanalysis.* London: Maresfield Library.

——— (1970). *Attention and Interpretation.* London: Maresfield Library.

Brabant, E., Falzeder, E., & Giampieri-Deutsch P. (Eds.) (1992). *The Correspondence of Sigmund Freud and Sandor Ferenczi—Volume 1, 1908–1914.* Cambridge, Massachusetts: The Belknap Press of Harvard University Press.

Caper, R. (1988). *Immaterial Facts.* Northvale, New Jersey: Jason Aronson.

Freud, S. (1893). Charcot. In J. Strachey (Ed. & Trans.). *The Standard Edition of the Complete Psychological Works of Sigmund Freud* (*Standard Edition*) (Vol. 3, pp. 7–23). London: Hogarth Press.

——— (1895). Project for a scientific psychology. *Standard Edition* (Vol. 1, pp. 281–397). London: Hogarth Press.

——— (1900). The interpretation of dreams. Part I & II. *Standard Edition* (Vols. 4 & 5). London: Hogarth Press.

——— (1909). Analysis of a phobia in a five-year-old boy. *Standard Edition* (Vol. 10, pp. 1–149). London: Hogarth Press.

——— (1911). Formulations on the two principles of mental functioning. *Standard Edition* (Vol. 12, pp. 213–226). London: Hogarth Press.

——— (1912). Recommendations to physicians practising psycho-analysis. *Standard Edition* (Vol. 12, pp. 109–120). London: Hogarth Press.

——— (1913). Totem and taboo. *Standard Edition* (Vol. 13, pp. 1–162). London: Hogarth Press.

——— (1914). On Narcissism: an introduction. *Standard Edition* (Vol. 14, pp. 67–102). London: Hogarth Press.

——— (1915a). Instincts and their vicissitudes. *Standard Edition* (Vol. .4, pp. 109–140). London: Hogarth Press.

——— (1915b). Repression. *Standard Edition* (Vol. 14, pp. 141–158). London: Hogarth Press.

——— (1915c). The unconscious. *Standard Edition* (Vol. 14, pp. 159–215). London: Hogarth Press..

——— (1915d). Thoughts for the times on war and death. *Standard Edition* (Vol. 14, pp. 273–302). London: Hogarth Press.

——— (1916). On transience. *Standard Edition* (Vol. 14, pp. 303–307). London: Hogarth Press.

——— (1916–1917). Introductory lectures on psycho-analysis. *Standard Edition* (Vols. 15 & 16). London: Hogarth Press.

——— (1917). Mourning and melancholia. *Standard Edition* (Vol. 14, pp. 237–260). London: Hogarth Press.

——— (1920). Beyond the pleasure principle. *Standard Edition* (Vol. 18, pp. 1–64). London: Hogarth Press.

——— & Breuer, J. (1895) Studies on hysteria. *Standard Edition* (Vol. 2, pp. 281–397). London: Hogarth Press.

Gay P. (1995). *Freud: A Life for our Time.* London: Papermac. (Original work published 1988).

Hale, N.G. (1995). *The Rise and Crisis of Psychoanalysis in the United States.* New York: Oxford University Press.

Holt, R. (1985). The current status of psychoanalytic theory. *Psychoanalytic Psychology* 2:289–315.

Jones, E. (1953). *Sigmund Freud: Life and Work. Vol. I: The Young Freud 1856–1900.* London: Hogarth Press.

——— (1955). *Sigmund Freud: Life and Work. Vol. 2: Years of Maturity 1901–1919.* London: Hogarth Press.

Klein, G. S. (1976). *Psychoanalytic Theory: An Exploration of Essentials.* New York: International Universities Press.

Makari, G. (2008). *Revolution in Mind: The Creation of Psychoanalysis.* Melbourne: Melbourne University Press.

Malcolm, J. (1997). *In the Freud Archives.* New York: New York Review of Books. (Original work published 1984).

Masson, J. M. (Ed.) (1985). *The Complete Letters of Sigmund Freud to Wilhelm Fliess 1887–1904.* Cambridge, Massachusetts: Belknap Press of Harvard University Press.

Meltzer, D. (1978). *The Kleinian development. Part I: Freud's clinical development.* Strath Tay, Perthshire: Clunie Press.

Ogden, T. H. (2005). *This Art of Psychoanalysis: Dreaming Undreamt Dreams and Interrupted Cries.* Hove, East Sussex: Routledge.

Pfeiffer, E. (Ed.) (1963). *Sigmund Freud and Lou Andreas-Salomé—Letters.* London: The Hogarth Press and the Institute of Psycho-Analysis.

Schimmel P. W. (2014). *Sigmund Freud's Discovery of Psychoanalysis: Conquistador and Thinker.* London: Routledge.

Searle, J. R (1998). *The Rediscovery of the Mind.* Cambridge, Massachusetts: MIT Press.

Strachey, J. (Ed.) (1957). Editor's note: Melancholia. *The Standard Edition of the Complete Psychological Works of Sigmund Freud* (Vol. 14, pp. 239–242). London: Hogarth Press.

All the rage: Bion, psychic destructiveness, and the 'death instinct'

Abstract

This paper addresses the centrality of psychic destructiveness in the psychoanalytic process, and the effect of the experience of World War I on both Sigmund Freud and Wilfred Bion. The theory of the 'death instinct' is critiqued. The reality and extent of human destructiveness are not in doubt, but the 'death instinct theory' is vulnerable to logical critique. It is neither provable nor falsifiable. The present paper is one in conceptual logic, and no clinical material is included, for the simple reason that clinical material is only evidence of the manifestations of human destructiveness, and cannot prove or disprove the activity of a death instinct. The etiology of human destructiveness may be interpreted either within the framework of the death instinct, or outside of this framework. Wilfred Bion employed the Kleinian death instinct theory in his early papers, but gradually seems to have moved away from this position, towards an alternative formulation of the constitutional factor in terms of the infant's capacity to tolerate frustration. In so doing he offered a way out of the 'death instinct' debate. Possible factors contributing to his shift are considered.

> It is a sign of weakness to combine empirical and logical arguments, for the latter if valid, make the former superfluous.
>
> (Bertrand Russell, 1946)

Patients come to psychoanalysis and psychotherapy because they cannot 'learn from experience', to use one of Bion's phrases. If they could do so they would avail themselves of their experiences and relationships in such a way as to grow and develop.

The psychotherapy patient is not simply a hungry person who can make use of food when it becomes available. The situation is more analogous to the person who has been starving for so long that their digestive system has shut down and can no longer make immediate use of food. The real problem is the psychic 'structure', or psychic way of functioning, that has become established in response to the period of 'starvation'. In the case of the psychotherapy patient, rather than a lack of actual food, we are probably dealing with a developmental experience where there was felt to be a starvation of thoughtful attention from another mind. A lack of actual food can, of course, also occur.

Bion speculated about a certain kind of patient who, out of frustration in early development, turns against emotional experience with hatred and attacks it. Emotional realities such as pain and rage are felt to be so intolerable that they must be evacuated or obliterated, and this includes obliteration of any awareness of the hatred itself. 'Fear, hate and envy are so feared that steps are taken to destroy awareness of all feelings, although this is indistinguishable from taking life itself' (Bion, 1962, p 10). Therapeutic progress with such a patient will depend upon the extent to which the forces against the experience of emotional reality can be transformed and become less potent.

How a person, any one of us, deals with feelings of hatred and rage has a great impact upon our mind and how we are able to use it. The 'splitting off' of such feelings from consciousness is often linked to a state of psychic impoverishment. A failure of abstraction, linked to the failure to develop Bion's hypothetical alpha-function ensues (ibid. p. 60). In summary Bion suggests, such an individual may have survived in life, but without really living; without awareness of L, H and K (ibid. p. 42). He or she is therefore confused between life and death, and unsure what either would really mean. On the other hand, the emergence of such powerful emotional experience and the attendant anxiety directly into consciousness, as a result of the 'containment' offered in a psychotherapeutic experience, can facilitate a process of 'transformation' and mark the beginning of new life.

Not infrequently, this emergence and experience of primitive anxieties and hatred in consciousness has the quality of an eruption. The eruption is explained by the strength, even violence, of the forces themselves, and the resistance to their emergence; just as the crust of the earth provides resistance to the emergence of the magma beneath, which may then break through in the form of an eruption. In the context of a therapeutic relationship, such an eruption of rage may sometimes be precipitated by an interpretation or action on the part of the analyst which pierces the patient's narcissism; that is, which pierces some protective, but isolating emotional barrier. The patient may then feel overwhelmed with a violent conscious hatred and anger, a wish to smash up everything and everybody, including of course the analyst, who will not be thanked for helping bring about this state of affairs. Nevertheless, such a development, if it can be survived, is potentially a step towards psychic integration.

In this paper I will only be able to cover part of what Bion had to say about human destructiveness and its origins. The first section of the paper deals with the impact of the First World War on both Freud's and Bion's theoretical thinking, as the experience was formative for both men. I will consider Freud's subsequent formulation of the theory of a 'death instinct'. The second parts of the paper are titled 'Controversy over the death instinct', and 'Death Instinct vs Death Anxiety', respectively. The third part, 'Wilfred Bion and the death instinct—The Kleinian influence', will consider Bion's initial attempts to conceptualize the origins of human destructiveness employing the Kleinian version of the 'death instinct'. The final part of the paper, 'Beginnings of a new theory', will consider Bion's development of his 'theory of thinking', and the new conceptualization of the origins of human destructiveness inherent in his emerging understanding of the mind.

World War I

When the First World War broke out Sigmund Freud was aged 58, and Wilfred Bion was 18. There were 40 years between them, and they were on opposite sides of the conflict. Freud had several sons involved in the fighting, although miraculously all were to survive. Bion joined the Tank Corps, and he also would, miraculously, survive. Their very different experiences of the war were to prove profoundly disillusioning for both, although the word 'disillusionment' would hardly seem to do justice to the horror of Bion's experience.

Until the First War Freud had managed to maintain something of the militaristic frame of mind that was reflected in his childhood idealizations of various military adventurers, particularly Hannibal and Napoleon. At the outbreak of the war Freud was optimistic for a swift victory by Austria and her allies. 'All my libido is given to Austro-Hungary', he said (Jones, 1953, Vol. 2, p 192). Freud's fantasy was of a passage of arms conducted in an essentially chivalrous manner. The man who had prided himself on his knowledge of what was primitive within the human mind, was simply not prepared for what was to come. But by 1915, in 'Thoughts for the times on war and death', he wrote:

> Then the war in which we had refused to believe broke out, and it brought—disillusionment... We welcome illusions because they spare us unpleasurable feelings, and enable us to enjoy satisfactions instead. We must not complain, then, if now and

> again they come into collision with some portion of reality, and are shattered against it.
>
> (Freud, 1915*b*, p 278 and p 280)

This experience of disillusion appears to have had a profound impact upon Freud's mind; it forced him to, and also freed him up to, confront the need to understand more about the nature of human destructiveness. The nature of the explanatory formulation that he came to, that is the death instinct, has remained one of the most contentious of his theoretical ideas. Although Freud's theory originated in his clinical experience, his formulation linked it to biological speculations. It is therefore not a purely psychoanalytic formulation, in contrast to 'Mourning and melancholia', for example (Schimmel, 2018). However, the important observation at this point is that Freud had been under the influence of an illusion.

In contrast, it seems that the young Wilfred Bion was to be disillusioned before he really had time to recognize he had any illusions in the first place. He was thrown into something beyond his comprehension, and like Freud his experience of the war would compel him to contemplate the problem of human destructiveness.

The first part of Bion's autobiography is titled 'The long week-end: 1897–1919' (Bion, 1982). It is an account of his childhood and life up until the end of the First World War, and although Bion links the events in a continuous narrative, it is the account of the war that comes to dominate the book. Clearly, Bion felt it was something he had to get out, and down on paper, before he died. Towards the end of the book, as he writes, he is pursued by the memory of being with a dying soldier 'Sweeting':

> These old ghosts, they never die. They don't even fade away; they preserve their youth wonderfully. Why, you can even see the beads

> of sweat, still fresh, still distinct, against the pallor of their brows. How is it done?
>
> (ibid. p 264)

These ghosts pursued him throughout his life.

Bion's account of the war is an extraordinarily honest document; we have a sense of being both inside his mind and in some way in the experience.

Bion was 19 or 20 years of age when he first saw action as a tank commander. Death was the constant companion. The tanks were death traps, and the tank commander's job was to direct the tanks from outside, on foot. In a late action of the war Bion's tanks are advancing but the supporting infantry attack does not materialize. Bion rushes back, 'Terrified at what would happen to the tanks without infantry support to keep enemy gunners immobilized', which was, he comments, 'a very slender hope at the best of times.' The infantry does not attack. Bion is now in a trench but too far away to get back to the tanks. He watches helplessly:

> The tanks rolled up a gentle grassy slope. There was a soft muffled explosion. Robertson's tank opened up as a flower in a nature film might unfold. Another thud, then two, almost simultaneous, followed. The whole four flowered. Hard, bright flames, as if cut out of tinfoil, flickered and died, extinguished by the bright sun.
>
> Like a boy learning a task set out for detention I repeated mentally, 'I must remember these four officers and all their men are dead.' I do not remember the slightest suspicion of mourning or regret.
>
> (ibid. p 254)

> The tanks had been ordered to attack at 10-30 am, a suicidal gesture. 'There were night attacks, dawn attacks, feint attacks; but not a 10-30 attack—surely not 10-30?' (ibid. p 256).

Assignment to the tanks was in effect a death sentence. The tank commanders were the only ones with any real chance of survival in the longer term. At the end of the war, of the battalion that Bion had begun with, only two combat officers, other than himself, remained, but '...of the men there was none. Even of those who had seen more than six months fighting there was a mere handful' (ibid. p 286). As Bion suggests, he is not sure whether he has survived the carnage and is still in the world. I am reminded of the anecdote of the patient brought to Bion in supervision: a man, who switched on the light at night to see if he was still in bed. Bion is purported to have said, 'Well, everyone is entitled to a second opinion' (N Symington, verbal communication). I imagine Bion could well identify with the man's dilemma.

The impact of Bion's war experience seems present in many of his subsequent conceptual formulations. The tanks themselves could be seen as a realization of his concept of the rigid crushing container. In another action, Bion, who is sick with a fever, finds himself having had to take over the command of a tank, so is inside, and directing the driver. He notices German observation balloons in the air. He had also noticed some artillery fire. He doesn't put two and two together immediately, until his driver says:

> 'It's those balloons sir.'
>
> Of course—it had not occurred to me! We were under direct observation; they must be concentrating on us....
>
> 'Get out!' I shouted. 'All of you! Walk close behind.' They tumbled out. I took over driving the tank, meaning to drive a zig-zag course with the escape hatch over me open. Then I realized that with no crew I could not steer the tank and could not drive anywhere but

> straight ahead. I had no sense of fear. I opened the throttle so the tank was at full speed.
>
> Before I knew what I was doing I had left the driver's seat and joined the crew behind. It was difficult to keep up with the fast-moving driverless tank. Then, only then, panic overwhelmed me. Suppose they were *not* firing at us? Suppose they did not hit us? A fully equipped tank in complete working order would have been handed over to the enemy, abandoned on my orders by its crew.
>
> I could not catch up with it; as I stumbled and tried to run to the door I fell. Then mercifully the shell hit, pierced and burst. The tank stopped, flames spurting everywhere. In a moment it was a total wreck.
>
> I felt bemused, unable to grasp what had happened. I only knew that I had failed in my desperate resolve to get back to the tank. Had I succeeded I could not possibly have survived.
>
> (ibid. p 262)

Bion does not point out the obvious, that if he had not ordered his crew out of the tank, no one would have survived. It is difficult not to think that the hard rigid physical reality of the tanks themselves, and of the authoritarian command mentality that sent tanks into action at 10-30 in the morning, did not shape Bion's concept of the hard, rigid or crushing container; the container that destroys the life of its contents (Souter, K.M., 2009).

My interpretation is that, at the moment Bion abandoned the tank, he was escaping from the rigid container we call authority, which is inimical to thinking. Bion writes he left the tank before he knew what he was doing. This episode is, I think, also a realization of his notion of 'thinking under fire'. Such a process might take place outside of the self that thinks it knows what it is doing; in this case, Bion would seem to have been following a process of intuitive 'commonsense' thinking, which placed collective survival above other considerations. It is important to note, it is not a self-centred concern for survival. The Symingtons, in their book on Bion, make the point that Bion's connection with the group was through thought, as opposed to the unthinking identification with the group (Symington, N and J, 1996 p. 19). The connection through thinking, that is real thinking, includes concern for the group. I think it is valid to interpret Bion's instructions to the crew to leave the tank as both a manifestation of concern and a breaking out of the unthinking identification with the group, by means of thinking.

It is also important to understand that Bion's concept of thinking does not refer to a purely cognitive process. In his theoretical work Bion took the innovative step of placing emotional experience at the centre of his conception of thinking.

Bion was haunted by the 'old ghosts' of the First War and had experienced for himself the separation of thinking from emotional experience that so often is a feature of trauma: 'I must remember these four officers and all their men are dead. I do not remember the slightest suspicion of mourning or regret.' His traumatic experience of the war drew his attention to the problems of the destruction of the thinking and feeling mind.

After demobilization he went on to train in medicine and psychiatry and became an army psychiatrist. During the Second World War he was involved with units dedicated to the rehabilitation of soldiers suffering war neuroses; probably a reflection of an on-going attempt to understand his own lingering state of 'shell shock'.

Before the Second World War, Bion had an experience of analysis with John Rickman, and after the Second War he sought a second analysis. It is perhaps not surprising that he chose Melanie Klein as his analyst; not only was it clear that she was at the 'cutting edge' of new thinking, but in the clinical encounter she would be concerned to understand the nature of the destructive forces within the mind.

Bion would qualify as a member of the British Society and, initially at least, was to some extent identified with the Kleinian group. According to Grosskurth, going into analysis with Klein, Bion had felt the need to emphasize that he would remain his own person (Grosskurth, 1985 p. 427). This he was able to do, but it seems to have taken him some time to arrive there.

Controversy over the death instinct

'The concept of the death instinct is one of the most controversial concepts in psychoanalysis' (Fayek, 1980 p. 447). 'Freud's concept of the "death instinct" is probably his least generally accepted and most controversial psychoanalytic idea' (Chessick, 1992 p 3).

I will concentrate here on writings that address the short comings of these theories. To my mind they are weak theories and logically flawed.

In *Beyond the pleasure principle*, Freud proposed the 'death instinct' or 'death drive', Thanatos, as a fundamental and innate disposition within the organism in opposition to the 'life instinct' or 'life drive', Eros (Freud, 1920*g*).

The 'death instinct' tends to divide psychoanalysts into camps. The 'Kleinians' accepted it, for example Michael Feldman (2000) follows up his interesting clinical material by invoking the death instinct to explain his patient's destructiveness. To my mind, the most powerful argument against the death instinct is that it acts as a distorting preconception. Ahumada's (2019) paper in the IPA's recent publication *The uncanny* ends with a thoughtful critique of Freud's 'death instinct', which as he says 'lends itself to too-ready use as an explanatory device' (p. 73).

The question I want to focus on is 'why'? Why should the personality, or particularly the psychotic part of the personality, come to possess such powerful destructive impulses in the first place?

Despite *Beyond the pleasure principle* possessing passages of imaginative and intuitive genius, Freud's argument seems, at times, to slip into conceptual incoherence. This is most evident when he invokes biology to back up his theory. Bolivar, a supporter of the concept of the death instinct suggests its truth has been 'obscured by his (Freud's) apparently unfortunate decision to formulate his daring discovery in biological terms' (1993 p. 124). Bolivar has suggested 'the theory of the death instinct, as it is expressed by Freud is in need of being radically reformulated, since it is both scientifically and philosophically unacceptable insofar as it was presented by Freud in dubious biological basis' (ibid. p. 123).

Otto Kernberg (2009) in a comprehensive paper on the death drive, comments on Freud's biological speculations in *Beyond the pleasure principle*: 'While it may be tempting to explain psychological functions by analogical ones from biology, this runs the risk of reductionism by relating complex phenomena at widely different structural levels to each other' (p. 1017). And, 'In conclusion, Freud's dramatic concept of the death drive may not reflect an inborn disposition as such, but is eminently relevant in clinical practice' (p. 1020).

Melanie Klein, based on her clinical observations, also emphasized the innate aggressive and destructive elements of the 'death instinct'. She juxtaposed the libidinal manifestations of the infant's emotional life, which she conceptualized as arising from the 'life instinct', to the aggressive and sadistic manifestations of the infant's emotional life, which she conceptualized as arising from the 'death instinct' (Klein, 1952). In this way, she seems to have regarded the 'death instinct' as possessing an innate drive component, in an opposite, but equivalent, sense to the way the manifestations of libido reflect the drive component of the 'life instinct'. I understand Klein's death instinct to constitute a dispositional state within the infant which contains 'drive' elements, so in this sense it is also linked to the biological constitution. I will call this the 'Klein version' of the death instinct. However, it is interesting to note, that her specific statements possibly allow a little room for ambiguity, as she repeatedly refers to death anxiety, and aggressive or sadistic 'impulses', rather than always to drives (Klein, 1952).

Klein would go on to hypothesize an innate and primitive envy present from birth, which seems to have been conceptualized either as a modified form of, or particular manifestation of, the 'death instinct' (Klein, 1957).

The death instinct may be reformulated as arising out of a 'death anxiety', rather than some inherent biological or inherent psychic reality. Bonasia writes, 'The hypothesis that suicide may also be the elaboration of a primary death anxiety of the fearful and uncontrollable event, is not considered' (by Freud) (1988 p. 284).

Death instinct vs death anxiety

Given the hatred and violence inherent in suicide, Bonasia's position may seem counter-intuitive. I think, however, a coherent argument can be mounted that the fundamental source of destructiveness begins with a death anxiety. Infantile anxiety about survival can lead to an attack on emotional experience, as suggested by Bion (1962 p. 10). For the infant, 'Fear, hate and envy are so feared that steps are taken to destroy awareness of all feelings, although that is indistinguishable from taking life itself.'

Grotstein believes the 'death instinct template contains a palimpsest of the history of the terrors all living and extinct organisms have endured. Its origins therefore lie in the genetic record of the human race. He conceives of the death instinct beginning as a death anxiety. It is not, suggests Grotstein, opposed to the life instinct, but exists as part of the life instinct, and in the service of life. He describes patients who, in his judgment, have experienced a 'mental death' or a death of the soul in terms of loss of innocence, in infancy or childhood. His view seems primarily object relational, without ignoring the instinctual endowment of the human organism. (2000 p. 473).

Kernberg has written that the question of, 'whether aggression is primary or a secondary response to trauma and frustration permeates the psychological field widely beyond psychoanalysis proper (2009 p. 1009). He continues:

> On the other hand, a pure drive theory that does not consider the specific vicissitudes of affects tends to acquire over-generalized and rigidly dogmatic aspects that also run counter to clinical experience: to explain unconscious conflict as simple struggles between libido and aggressive drives does not do justice to the complexity of clinical experience (p. 1010).

Kernberg appears to regard the death drive as an evocative descriptive term for human destructiveness in certain individuals, but as a doubtful etiological proposition.

> The death drive, I propose, is not a primary drive, but represents a significant complication of aggression as a major motivational system ... and as such is eminently useful as a concept in the clinical realm (p. 1017).

Biernoff (1952) seems to challenge Levin's (1951) critique of Freud's death instinct and summarizes Levin's argument:

> Levin's thesis is that Freud's death instinct is an absurd concept and was originated by Freud as a reaction to his fear and rejection of life. Freud, he claims, instead of recognizing the origin of those fears in his own Oedipus complex, projected them on Nature, Fate and Mankind. Death as inorganic peace was Freud's method of pacifying a cruel world of terrors. (Biernoff, 1952 p. 275)

Black (2001), in a detailed analysis of possible reasons for Freud's arriving at the concept of the Death Drive, points out Freud's ambivalence and his self-effacing comments in 'Beyond the Pleasure Principle'.

> Freud 'warns us in advance that what we will meet is 'speculation, often far-fetched speculation' (1920 p. 24). He puts his position that: 'I am not convinced myself and that I do not seek to persuade other people to believe in them…' (1920 p. 59).

Black (2001) suggests that Freud supported his claims using 'a rather surprising argument from evolution' and 'came to support it with a neuroanatomical argument dating back to the earliest days of psychoanalysis.' (p. 185)

Freud's claim to have followed a line of thought is misleading suggests Black:

> In fact, however, he has not really followed a line of thought: he has made a speculative leap, and in view of the odd echoes between style and subject-matter, the reader may wonder if Freud is not writing at this point in a manner more akin to that of a poet than a scientist.
>
> (Black p. 187)

At the end of his paper Black's conclusion is: 'The death drive, as such, probably merits no future in psychoanalytic thinking.' (p. 195

It seems that Wilfred Bion in his early writings accepted the idea but later shifted away from it.

In the 1950's Bion published a series of individual papers, which would later be collected together and republished in 1967 as *Second thoughts*. In a number of these papers he describes his attempts to pursue clinical psychoanalytic work with a number of very disturbed schizophrenic and psychotic patients. Herbert Rosenfeld and Hanna Segal were also attempting to undertake such work with psychotic patients. All of them seemed to have employed Klein's theory of the failure to achieve the psychic integration characteristic of what she called the 'depressive position'. As a consequence, such patients were thought to remain in the so-called 'paranoid-schizoid' position, or mode of functioning. All were in agreement that one of the factors behind this failure of psychic integration was, as Bion puts it, 'a preponderance of destructive impulses'. In the schizophrenic, says Bion, there is a 'preponderance of destructive impulses so great that even the impulses to love are suffused by them and turned to sadism.' Bion had seen enough to be under no illusions about the possibility of a human mind coming under the sway of a 'preponderance of destructive impulses' (Bion, 1967 p. 37). He was also in analysis with Melanie Klein and we might guess attempting to form some awareness of destructive processes within himself.

At this time, Bion conceptualized the process of psychic integration that leads out of the unintegrated 'paranoid schizoid' position into the 'depressive position', as dependent on a process of linking together of elements within the mind. However, excessive destructiveness leads to 'attacks on linking' (Bion, 1967, p 93) and prevents this process of integration. A realistic appraisal of both external reality and intrapsychic reality cannot then be achieved. The concept of 'attacks on linking' was central to Bion's early thinking about destructive forces within the mind. It was to remain so, appearing in different transformations over time, such as '-K' and 'reversal of *a* function'.

Bion (1967) wrote of the process of divergence of the psychotic personality from the non-psychotic personality, and in so doing was referring both to the possible difference between two separate persons, but also to the possibility of there being two such 'personalities' within each of us. He suggested that the potentially psychotic personality is burdened by the 'preponderance of destructive impulses', and this leads to a 'hatred of reality' which, 'as Freud pointed out, is extended to all aspects of the psyche that make for awareness of it.' Bion adds that there is also a 'hatred of internal reality and all that makes for awareness of it' (p. 37).

Because the functions of perception are necessary for the apprehension of reality, whether internal or external, Bion suggested that the functions of the perceptual organs themselves can come under attack from the psychotic personality. This he understood to be the origin of the hallucinatory disturbances which occur in psychotic states. Reality is hated and obliterated along with the perceptual functions which could potentially allow a greater apprehension of reality (1967 p. 38).

Likewise, the capacity for verbal thought, which is intimately linked with conceptual thinking and self-awareness, also comes under attack. This is seen as linked to the disorganization of conceptual thought and the delusions which occur in psychotic states (1967, p 48).

In 'Notes on a theory of schizophrenia' Bion commented:

> From the patient's point of view the achievement of verbal thought has been a most unhappy event. Verbal thought is so interwoven with catastrophe and the painful emotion of depression, that the patient, resorting to projective identification, splits it off and pushes it into the analyst. The results are again unhappy for the patient; lack of this capacity is now felt by him to be the same thing as being

> insane. On the other hand, resumption of this capacity seems to him to be inseparable from depression and awareness, on a reality level this time, that he is "insane".
>
> (Bion 1967, p 32)

Bion's initial position was more or less in line with the conception of an innate and constitutional factor as hypothesized by Klein in her version of the 'death instinct'. In his paper 'The development of schizophrenic thought' he wrote: 'Melanie Klein believes that this conflict (between life and death instincts) persists throughout life, and this view I believe to be of great importance to an understanding of the schizophrenic' (Bion, 1967 p 36). While Bion's early statements seem to put the emphasis on constitutional endowment rather than the environment in the genesis of schizophrenia, for the most part he left room for ambiguity, and he was also often ambiguous as to how he conceptualized the nature of the constitutional endowment.

In 'Attacks on linking', one of the later papers published in the series in *Second thoughts*, Bion paid greater attention to the 'environmental' factor. He speculated about the maternal failure to be receptive to the infant's means of communication and the deleterious effect for the infant. However, having introduced this environmental factor, he adds the following qualification:

> I do not put forward this experience as the cause of the patient's disturbance; that finds its main source in the inborn disposition of the infant… the inborn characteristics and the part that they play in producing attacks by the infant on all that links him to the breast, namely, primary aggression and envy.
>
> (Bion 1967, p 105)

At this point it would seem Bion is specifying the nature of the inborn characteristics he is referring to as 'primary aggression and envy.'

This is the one statement I have come across in Bion's writings which seems unambiguously supportive of what I have called the 'Klein version' of the death instinct. For Bion, with his philosophical background, I think the adoption of the Klein version is surprising, and I will say more about why. It was, however, a position that he gradually moved away from, and I am not aware of similar passages placing such emphasis on the innate and primary aspects of aggression and envy in his writings subsequent to 'Attacks on linking'.

Beginnings of a new theory

The evolution of Bion's thinking is, I think, particularly helpful in that it offers us a coherent way out of the 'death instinct' debate. We might say Bion took the argument 'beyond the death instinct', and back to the pleasure principle. I will attempt to make clear why this is so.

To turn to the final paper in *Second thoughts*, called 'A theory of thinking', and also Bion's early book, *Learning from experience*: in these works he hypothesizes the essential elements of his theory of mind, and how he conceptualizes that the development of thinking comes about, or fails to come about, as the case may be.

In *Learning from experience* Bion refers to Freud's two principles of mental functioning, the pleasure principle and the reality principle. Freud's hypothesis was that the pleasure principle is fundamental and acts in an immediate way to seek out what is felt to be pleasurable and avoid what is felt to be painful. The reality principle however, is that capacity, which Freud suggests develops over time, by which the organism can defer immediate gratification in order to accommodate to the demands of reality and thereby achieve a more satisfactory adaptation to reality in the longer term. The reality principle presumes an inhibition of motor discharge and a capacity to wait. Bion refers to Freud:

> Restraint of motor discharge (of action) had now become necessary and was provided by means of the process of *thought*, which was developed from ideation. Thought was endowed with qualities which made it possible for the mental apparatus to support increased tension during a delay in the process of discharge. It is essentially an experimental way of acting…
>
> (Bion, 1962 p.28)

Bion points out that it is implicit in Freud's statement that this restraint of motor action, the delay in 'discharge' as Freud puts it, is dependent upon the organism's capacity to tolerate frustration. 'The link between intolerance of frustration and the development of thought is central to an understanding of thought and its disturbances' (ibid. p 29).

We might characterize the difference as between a 'reaction' to something which is automatic and born of the 'pleasure principle', and a 'response' to something which involves thinking and is born of the 'reality principle'.

Bion speculates about the situation of the newborn infant which he uses to build a model for the processes of mental development. The first experiences at the breast were also, of course, where Melanie Klein's speculations took her in trying to understand the development of the mind, but we see Bion's conceptual speculation is subtle, and more complex.

The newborn infant, he suggests, requires the breast/mother to supply both milk and love:

> The 'breast is an object the infant needs to supply it with milk and good internal objects. I do not attribute to the infant an awareness of this need; but I do attribute to the infant an awareness of a need

> not satisfied. We can say the infant feels frustrated if we assume the existence of some apparatus with which frustration can be experienced. Freud's concept of consciousness as that of "a sense-organ for the perception of psychical qualities", provides such an apparatus.'
>
> (Bion 1962, p 34)

Here Bion initiated a crucial conceptual move by distinguishing between a need, and a need not satisfied; it is the need not satisfied that potentially leads to awareness. He further develops his train of thought by making the logical point that if, at the very beginning, no conception of a good breast has yet developed, the awareness in question cannot be awareness of the need for a 'good breast' missing, but rather will be experienced as a persecutory awareness, that of a 'bad breast' present', (which we call a 'bad object'). '...the infant does not feel it wants a good breast but it does feel it wants to evacuate a bad one' (ibid. p 34).

So, as Bion points out, the so-called 'bad breast' experience must precede the 'good breast' experience; in the beginning the taking in of milk will be experienced as '...indistinguishable from evacuating a bad breast.' It will take the infant some time to establish the '... "idea of a breast missing" and not as a bad breast present' (ibid. p 34). Satisfactory experiences of feeding and love will be necessary, in order to establish in the mind the idea of a 'good breast' that can provide for the infant's needs and can also then be felt to be missing. The infant's initial experience of hunger will be weighted to that of a persecutory 'bad breast' or 'bad object'. There will be an urgent pressure or need to get rid of, or evacuate, this 'bad breast'. Optimally this is accomplished in a satisfactory feeding experience. The same argument can be extended to any unmet physical and /or emotional need of the infant; such a need would presumably become increasingly persecutory the longer it remains unmet.

We know that a newborn infant seeks out the mother's breast, and clearly therefore has some sort of template in the mind representing the breast experience. Bion calls this template of a breast that can provide, a 'preconception' (1963 p 23). We cannot know exactly what constitutes this 'preconception', but it is innate. In Bion's view, it seems not to constitute a form of awareness. Bion suggests such a preconception can evolve, if matched with an appropriate realization, into a conception of a breast. That is, experiences of the breast lead to development from the preconception to the conception 'breast', and it will take repeated 'good enough' experiences of the breast for the conception of a 'good breast' to evolve.

In his paper 'A theory of thinking' Bion first introduced his crucial idea of the capacity to tolerate frustration. He posed the question as to what might happen for an infant whose expectation of a breast is matched, or mated, as he puts it, with an experience of no breast available. In the face of this 'bad breast' experience what happens will depend on the infant's capacity to tolerate frustration. If the capacity to tolerate frustration is sufficient, suggests Bion, the 'no breast' experience becomes what he calls a 'thought'. Again, Bion refers to Freud's 'Two principles of mental functioning':

> If the capacity for toleration of frustration is sufficient...This initiates the state, described by Freud in his Two Principles of Mental Functioning, in which dominance by the reality principle is synchronous with the development of an ability to think and so to bridge the gulf of frustration between the moment when a want is felt and the moment when action appropriate to satisfying the want culminates in its satisfaction.
>
> (Bion, 1967 p. 112)

We can see from this idea that experiences of frustration which can be tolerated by the developing mind, are a potent force in the development of thoughts, and also of consciousness.

On the other hand, incapacity to tolerate frustration tips the balance in favour of the evasion of reality. When frustration cannot be tolerated, and the preconception 'breast' is met with an absence, then the experience of the 'bad object' is felt to be intolerable. It then has to be evaded through some means of 'evacuation'. Instead of the absent breast becoming a 'negative realization' leading to a thought, this situation fosters the development of a mind which has to substitute the evacuation of a 'bad breast' for the sought for 'good breast' experience. Bion suggested,

> The end result is that all thoughts are treated as if they were indistinguishable from bad internal objects; the appropriate machinery is felt to be, not an apparatus for thinking thoughts, but an apparatus for ridding the psyche of accumulations of bad internal objects.
>
> (ibid. p. 112)

Things are not always so black and white, and Bion also suggested an in-between possibility: 'If intolerance of frustration is not so great as to activate the mechanisms of evasion and yet is too great to bear the dominance of the reality principle, the personality develops omnipotence as a substitute…' and, 'This involves the assumption of omniscience as a substitute for learning from experience by aid of thoughts and thinking' (ibid. p 114).

At this point therefore, Bion was proposing a model for the development of the mind dependent both upon the quality of the environment, and the constitutional disposition of the infant. The environmental factors will depend, in particular, on the quality of care provided by the mother, or her surrogate. A crucial dimension of this environment will be the level of deprivation or the trauma the infant is exposed to. The constitutional factor is now conceptualized in terms of the capacity of the infant to tolerate frustration of its needs. This innate capacity, or lack of capacity, to deal with frustration will be a crucial factor, just as the mother's capacity to help her infant manage its frustrations will prove a crucial factor. We can see that the two factors in the equation will in fact be intimately related to each other and are interacting right from birth. For example, even an infant with considerable capacity to tolerate frustration is likely to come to grief, if the mother is neglectful or is unable to communicate to her baby her concern and love; or, conversely, an infant with a very limited capacity to tolerate frustration, may be helped by a sensitive mother to manage its emotional experience and achieve a satisfactory psychic integration.

Bion's new formulation replaces the innate factor, as conceptualized in terms of the 'death instinct', with an innate factor conceptualized in terms of the capacity to tolerate frustration.

It seems somewhat surprising that Bion, with his philosophical gift, should have, for a time, adopted the 'Klein version' of the death instinct; that is the concept of a 'death instinct' as including the idea of primary and innate aggression and envy. Attribution of the constitutional component in human destructiveness, in whole or in part, to such a 'death instinct' would seem to be an extremely weak scientific theory. If we consider the 'Klein version', it would seem logically impossible to accrue unequivocal evidence in support of the theory. An instinctual force is known indirectly through its manifestations, so while any and all evidence of the human propensity for destructiveness is compatible with the 'death instinct' theory of causality, it is hard to see how any such evidence can favour this theory as against a plausible formulation of another hypothetical constitutional factor.

Newborns do have differing 'constitutions'. If we accept the likelihood that there is a constitutional factor contributing to the manifestations of human destructiveness, Bion has offered an alternative formulation of this constitutional factor in terms of the capacity to tolerate frustration. The lack of such a capacity would predispose to excessive frustration, which would in turn potentially generate experiences of anger and impulses of hatred. Clearly, Bion's hypothesis is conceptually distinct from the idea of an aggressive or destructive drive generated de novo from within the organism. Bion's new formulation does not rely on the introduction of the additional hypothetical factor of an independent inner drive that is the 'death instinct'. As such it has an economy and plausibility which the drive version of the 'death instinct' lacks. In science, a simple theory, so long as it has explanatory power equal to, or better than, another more complex theory, is clearly to be preferred.

However, to my mind, the greatest problem with the theory of the death instinct is not the difficulty of identifying supportive evidence, but rather the fact that the theory seems untestable, and therefore unfalsifiable. In *The logic of scientific discovery* Karl Popper has proposed the test of falsifiability as the crucial demarcation criterion for any theory to be considered scientific (Popper, 1959 p. 78*ff*). To simplify Popper's position, he suggested that if a theory is to be judged to be a scientific theory at all, it must be possible to conceptualize ways in which the theory may be put to the test and potentially shown to be false.

Popper, in fact has suggested that all psychoanalytic theory is unfalsifiable, however this challenge of Popper's to psychoanalysis is not of the essence in relation to Freud's 'death instinct', which appears to be a biological constitutional, rather than a purely psychoanalytic, theory. But whatever kind of theory it is, how would one disprove it?

Within the theoretical framework of the Klein version, the problem is that the operation of the 'death instinct' is proved by the presence of its manifestations, such as those of human destructiveness and envy. No matter what evidence might be adduced to support an alternative formulation of the origin of these manifestations, the advocate of the 'death instinct' can simply assert that none of this contradicts the operation of the innate 'death instinct' as a contributing and necessary factor. Within the theory, the 'death instinct' is a given, true by definition, and in this context, it is difficult to see how it could be disproved.

I would suggest that a theory for which we have no unequivocal supportive evidence on the one hand and, which does not admit tests of falsifiability on the other, is no theory at all; it is an empty idea, in the omniscient sense that Bion describes, and he should have known this. We don't know why, for a while, Bion embraced the idea of the death instinct. The obvious conjecture is that he was under the emotional sway of his analytic experience and relationship with Melanie Klein and it would take him time to reach a more independent position. His commenting that he would remain his own person in analysis with Klein perhaps suggests he was aware of a vulnerability in this regard. I also don't know if he ever refuted the idea of the Kleinian death instinct outright, but it is clear that he went beyond it.

Since submitting a preliminary version of this paper, I have come across a similar formulation to what I have proposed in the writings of philosopher Richard Wollheim. In his paper 'Emotion and the Malformation of Emotion' (1999), Wollheim suggests that destructive emotions are malformed emotions. 'For my suggestion is that envy, as Klein postulates it, is very close to my understanding of a malformed emotion'. And 'something on which Klein's Text (Envy and Gratitude) is not explicit is whether envy is an immediate response to satisfaction or frustration, or whether her belief is that something else has to intervene. I put the point thus because the account that I have offered of malformed emotion does, it will be recognized, introduce an intervening condition: the person's inability to accept satisfaction or frustration of desire is an intervening condition' (p. 129).

Bion returned to the so-called pleasure principle and the organism's inability to tolerate frustration, in order to formulate a more plausible account of the innate factors which shape the development of the mind.

References

Ahumada, G. (2019). On Freud's 'The Uncanny'. In C Bronstein & C Seulin (Eds.). *Contemporary Freud, Turning Points & Critical Issues* series, International Psychoanalytic Association.

Bion, W. (1998). *Learning from experience.* New Jersey: Jason Aronson (Original work published 1962).

——— (1989). *Elements of Psychoanalysis.* London: Karnac. (Original work published 1963).

——— (1993). *Second Thoughts.* London: Karnac. (Original work published 1967).

——— (1991). *The Long Week-end 1897–1919: Part of a Life.* London: Karnac. (Original work published 1982)

Black, D.M. (2001). Mapping a detour: why did Freud speak of a death drive? *British Journal of Psychotherapy* 18(2):185–198.

Bolivar, E. (1993). The ontological grounds of the death instinct in Freud. *Psychoanalysis and Contemporary Thought* 16(1):123–147.

Bonasia, E. (1988). Death instinct or fear of death? Research into the problem of death in psychoanalysis. *Rivista di Psicoanalisi*, 34(2):272–314.

Fayek, A. (1980). From interpretation to the death instinct. *International Review of Psychoanalysis* 7:447–457.

Feldman, M. (2000). Some views on the manifestation of the death instinct in clinical work. *International Journal of Psychoanalysis* 81(1):53–65.

Freud, S. (1915*b*). Thoughts for the times on war and death. In J. Strachey (Ed. & Trans.). *The Standard Edition of the Complete Psychological Works of Sigmund Freud* (Vol. 14, p. 275). London: Hogarth Press.

——— (1920*g*). Beyond the pleasure principle. *The Standard Edition of the Complete Psychological Works of Sigmund Freud,* (Vol. 18, p. 7).

Grosskurth P. (1985). *Melanie Klein: Her World and Her Work.* London: Hodder and Stoughton.

Grotstein, J.S. (2000). Some considerations of 'hate' and a reconsideration of the death instinct. *Psychoanalytic Inquiry* 20(3):462–480.

Jones, E. (1953). *Sigmund Freud: Life and Work* (Vols. 1–3). London: Hogarth Press.

Kernberg, O. (2009). The concept of the death drive: a clinical perspective. *International Journal of Psychoanalysis.* 90(5):1009–1023.

Klein, M. (1988). *Envy and Gratitude and Other Works 1946–1963.* London: Virago Press. (Original works published 1952 & 1957).

Popper, K. (1959). *The Logic of Scientific Discovery.* London: Hutchinson.

Russell, B. (1946). *A History of Western Philosophy.* London: George Allen & Unwin.

Schimmel P. (2018). Freud's selected fact: his journey of mourning. *International Journal of Psychoanalysis* 99(1): 208–229.

Souter, K.M. (2009). The War Memoires: some origins of the thought of W.R. Bion. *International Journal of Psychoanalysis* 90(4):795–808.

Symington, J. & N. (1996). *The Clinical Thinking of Wilfred Bion.* Routledge, London.

Wollheim, R. (1999). Emotion and the malformation of emotion. In D. Bell (Ed.) *Psychoanalysis and Culture: A Kleinian Perspective* (p. 122–135). London: Duckworth.

'Outside of time': free associations from the Antipodes

Outside of Time previously published in *The Australasian Journal of Psychotherapy*, Vol. 27, 2008; also published in *The Annual Bulletin of the British Psychoanalytical Society*, Vol. 4, 2014

Australia has a number of different species of cockatoos, but here in Sydney the sulphur-crested variety are the noisiest. Big pure white birds with a wedge of sulphur yellow crest feathers which spring up when they are anxious, agitated, aggressive, or just intrigued. With their characteristic gravelly squawk, they are raucous and rumbustious. Gregarious birds, they have unmistakable capacities for play and provocation.

Across the road from my analyst's rooms was a park frequented by the local gang of cockatoos. One day they were especially noisy. I commented that they seemed such 'timeless' birds. 'Outside of time' came the suggestion from behind the couch. That felt right, time just didn't seem a relevant dimension.

The phrase lodged in my mind, eventually shaping itself into a short poem:

Outside of time

White fragments of alarm,
the fleeting cockatoos
beat and weave

mending the rent air.
They flock and forget.
Looking out from nowhere
they dream blue-gums,
red earth, the blue vault above.
Outside of time, tilting
toward oblivion, always
they are searching
for themselves; their own
unbearable whiteness.

A poem perhaps about psychoanalysis, that peculiar indefinable process which, in many ways, resides outside of time. As far as I understand the thinking of Wilfred Bion, he seems to suggest that if we are searching for 'invariants', psychoanalytic 'truths', the noumenon, 'O', we will need to be looking somewhere outside our known space-time dimensions.

Paradoxically we also expect analysis to confer a sharper awareness of the passage of time, and 'training' analyses these days, at least in Australia, tend to be lengthy undertakings. The person who 'finishes' is probably a different one from the person who began, and a decade or more of a lifetime will have passed in the process. We are likely to be left with an acute sense of time passed, and opportunities gone.

I came to Australia from New Zealand with the hope of pursuing psychoanalytic training, which wasn't, and still isn't, available in New Zealand. Now, with an established life and practice in Sydney, and involvement in our local Sydney Institute for Psycho-Analysis, it has become difficult to find a way back 'home', yet I will always feel something of an outsider here in Australia. But perhaps, as a witness to the stories of others, the position of outsider is to some extent inevitable for a psychoanalyst.

Australia, at least as a colony of Great Britain, came into being as a land of 'outsiders' and in many respects remains so even today. Characterized by Robert Hughes (1988) as a 'fatal shore' for that first wave of arrivals; the convicts transported, in the hope of purging Britain of its criminal class, to a *terra nullius*, out of sight and mind on the other side of the globe. With the convicts came their gaolers, and a whole mercantile and administrative structure; a new colony was established. Successive waves of arrivals soon followed: adventurers and gold diggers, outback farmers and entrepreneurs, and since the Second World War the 'multicultural' influx of migrants from all parts of the world, especially Asia in recent years, and increasingly asylum seekers and refugees, today. Many of those who have made Australia home will have, to varying degrees, some 'trauma of dislocation' (Akhtar, 2007 p. 165) in their personal or family history. In this process of colonization, the only true insiders, Australia's Aboriginal people, with a culture dating back more than 40,000 years, have tragically become the most dispossessed, and in this sense the greatest 'outsiders' of all. Under the impact of an aggressive alien culture many would seem to have lost touch with their 'Dreaming'. For the Aborigines, Dreaming was a lived reality; for us today the word denotes an intriguing concept of a collective cultural reality 'outside of time'.

So, how has psychoanalysis fared in the space-time of this 'New World' down under; the antipode of Great Britain?

Cultural historian Joy Damousi notes that upon the establishment of the Melbourne Institute for Psychoanalysis in 1940, Melbourne's *Sun* newspaper reported: ' "Europe's loss is Australia's gain" ', and 'The *Sun* was full of praise for its director, the Hungarian psychoanalyst Clara Lazar-Geroe, one of the founders of the institute and "one of the world's 25 most distinguished child analysts".' (Damousi, 2005 p. 179).

'I came to Australia because Hitler came to Europe', said Geroe in an interview in 1977 (quoted in Hooke, 2010). However, her arrival in Australia had also been the outcome of considerable determination and hard work on the part of Ernest Jones and several Australian figures, in particular the Sydney psychiatrist and psychoanalyst Roy Winn (ibid. p. 180). Winn had trained with the British Society, before returning to Australia in 1931 (Thomson Salo, 2011 p. 346). While the United States received a steady stream of refugee analysts from Europe in the years leading up to the Second World War and following, Australia would initially receive only a few. Its 'White Australia policy' appears to have been a contributing factor; migrants other than the British were mostly excluded. The policy would not begin to shift until after the Second World War. Apparently, in 1938 six analysts applied to come to Australia, five Hungarian and one German. Only two of the Hungarians received a visa, Clara Geroe and Andrew Peto. Peto would not arrive until 1949 (Hooke, 2010). He became head of the Sydney Institute for Psychoanalysis established in 1951, but eventually decided to leave Australia in 1955, apparently as a result of the Australian government's failure to recognize his qualifications (Damousi, 2005 p. 195).

The five Hungarians had in fact previously applied to migrate to New Zealand but, recalled Geroe in 1977, 'with all the assistance from Jones, Princess Bonaparte and leading medical people in New Zealand, we were twice refused.' (quoted in Hooke, 2010). So, if fate had ordered things differently, there might have been a psychoanalytic training established in New Zealand today.

In order to make training possible in Australia, Ernest Jones arranged for Geroe to be accredited training analyst status within the British Society, and Melbourne was authorized to function as a branch of the Society (Hooke, 2010). It has, however, been suggested that Jones's motives were not entirely straightforward; that he was particularly keen on the Hungarians migrating to the Antipodes because he did not wish them to bring the Ferenczi influence to London! (ibid.)

In order to train candidates, Clara Geroe would be obliged to act as analyst, supervisor and teacher (Thomson Salo, 2011 p. 347). It was an arrangement broadly compatible with her own experienced Hungarian model of training, but fraught with potential problems.

Training became possible in Sydney briefly, during the time Andrew Peto was available as training analyst, but could not be sustained after his departure. Then, in 1958, Harry Southwood, an analysand of Clara Geroe, moved to Adelaide, and training also began there (Hooke, 2010). Up until this time the British Society had remained responsible for training in Australia, but the three centres were developing somewhat distinctive and differing psychoanalytic cultures, and disagreements became problematic. In 1967 the British Society would hand the task of supervising training over to the IPA, and in 1968 a 'Sponsoring Committee' from the IPA visited Australia in order to establish standards for training and facilitate progress towards Provisional Society status. Finally, in 1973 the Australian Psychoanalytical Society (APAS) was approved as a component society of the IPA at the Paris Congress (Thomson Salo, 2011 p. 349).

Distance and geographical isolation were probably factors contributing to the problematic differences in perspective and approach, which continued to develop and led to threatened splits between the now three IPA accredited training centres, Adelaide, Melbourne, and Sydney. The resulting conflicts became intense and would eventually lead to two site visiting committees from the IPA (ibid. p. 350). It was the last of these in 1986, consisting of Dr Arnold Cooper from the United States and Professor Joseph Sandler from Britain, which, working in conjunction with the local groups, was eventually successful in beginning to restore a measure of unity. A new constitution for the APAS as a federation of three branches, Adelaide, Melbourne, and Sydney, was established. The overall responsibility for training would henceforth rest with the Executive Committee of the APAS (ibid. p. 351). Cooper and Sandler also identified a stultifying authoritarian culture of conformity within the APAS, and suggested a series of measures to address these problems. If their site report is to be believed, in 1986 the APAS was very much restricted by what Australian 'bush poet' Banjo Paterson had described as the 'yoke/ of staid conservancy' (see below).

The enthusiasm of the Melbourne *Sun* journalist at the arrival of Clara Geroe on Australian shores in 1940 was presumably hardly representative of public opinion. The stereotype Australian of that time was the practical man or woman, a do-it-yourself, 'Jack-of-all-trades', or Jill of the homestead, still imbued with the pioneering spirit of the first adventurers and colonist settlers. 'Mateship' was the doctrine of solidarity and identity which had grown up amongst Australian men, and which, with its equivalent ethos among Australian women, would prove a serviceable enough value system for the coming war.

Such men and women tended to be self-sufficient and stubborn, with a highly ambivalent attitude towards authority, and an irreverent, sceptical approach towards the supposed 'expert'. In his 1902 poem *The old Australian ways*, Banjo Paterson captured this ambivalence towards the 'home country':

> The narrow ways of English folk
> Are not for such as we;
> They bear the long-accustomed yoke
> Of staid conservancy:

The 'ordinary' self-sufficient Australian would hardly have been likely to perceive the relevance of a psychoanalyst to themselves and their way of life. Despite the enthusiasm of the *Sun* journalist, presumably the vast majority of people remained unaware of, and indifferent to, such developments.

There were of course those who did take an interest and, as in most parts of the world, Australia had its vigorous advocates, vigorous critics, and some virulent detractors, of Freudian psychoanalysis. From the outset,

Australian Psychiatry appears to have established an ambivalent relationship with psychoanalysis leaning to the negative, a situation not much changed today, except if anything the current climate is more hostile than ever. Psychoanalysis in Australia would remain something of a Cinderella; perhaps fortunately it never 'enjoyed' a period of institutionalized popularity within mainstream psychiatry, as it did in the United States.

Despite the 'conservancy' of the past, today a certain independence of mind may be found amongst those drawn from varying different backgrounds to our training. Perhaps this is in part a consequence of the fact that psychoanalysis in Australia has avoided popularization, and the absence of a mainstream and institutionalized culture of psychoanalysis within psychiatry. Certainly, our training is not generally regarded as a pathway to recognition and status within psychiatry, nor within clinical psychology.

Over the years the APAS has drawn its candidates and members from amongst psychiatrists, psychologists, and psychotherapists from a variety of different backgrounds and trainings. Membership has very slowly increased until the present, and today the APAS has between 70 and 80 active members and about 20 candidates in training. If, in the history of the APAS, geographical separation between the three training centres has been linked to a degree of difference in conceptions of the principles and practice of psychoanalysis, such differences constitute less of a problem today. There has been a long-standing practice of all candidates in training meeting three times a year as a group, once in each of the centres, Adelaide, Melbourne, and Sydney; our so-called 'Interstate weekends'. Possibly the Society is now enjoying the benefits of this on-going attempt to facilitate the building of relationships amongst the candidate groups, and other initiatives towards establishing a more coherent working group.

As T.S. Eliot has emphasized, an individual talent cannot flourish outside a creative and intellectual tradition (Eliot, 1919). Today, most Australian psychoanalysts would, I think, continue to see our tradition as lying within that of British psychoanalysis and our links as being with the British Society. However, a more local and independent 'tradition' may be beginning to flourish, and if a distinctive Antipodean position is to be identified, I think this might be characterized as the reluctance of many members to assume the mantle of any particular 'identification', whether with a theoretician, theoretical position, or group: 'Freudian', 'Kleinian', 'Winnicottian', 'Bionian', even the so-called 'independent' position. In recent times there would seem to be a movement away from attachments of identification. Attachment to, as opposed to relationship with, any psychoanalytic theory or 'school' perhaps inevitably compromises individual talent and creativity. If, first of all, we remain searching for ourselves, this is as it should be.

In thinking about what I might write by way of a perspective from Australia, I read with interest the previous contribution to this 'News from Around the World' series: 'Minding the Gap in Changed Times: A View from Afar-Buenos Aires, Argentina', by Jorge L. Ahumada (2013). I also read the previous Bulletin articles on BPAS issues cited by Ahumada: 'Reflections on the Present Condition of the British Psychoanalytical Society' by Michael Rustin (2012), and 'Thoughts about the Critical State of our Society' by Philip Stokoe (2012). The problems of a 'diminished availability of intensive psychoanalytic work and the decrease of candidates' (Ahumada, 2013 p. 41), are also, of course, realities we are having to face in Australia. It is however of interest to note, that despite an apparently diminished availability of patients seeking intensive work, our candidates continue to be able to find training cases meeting the minimum requirement of attending four times a week, albeit with some difficulty at times.

As in many countries in the world, Australian psychoanalysts are rubbing the sleep from their eyes as we wake out of a dreamless slumber; the assumption that our institutions will survive and thrive if we continue with business as usual. Voices amongst us, in particular past president of our society, Maria Teresa Hooke, have been pointing out that we face a potential crisis of aging, but for many of us in Sydney at least, the reality of our local situation was only fully grasped as the result of a presentation to our Institute about two years ago by Dr Mark Howard. His presentation, 'Thinking while Sinking', spelt out the local demographic realities of our aging membership, including of course training analysts, and also an older candidate group. In Sydney, we are not yet faced with a definite decline in numbers of candidates training, however taking into account the overall ages of members and candidates, the number of candidates currently being trained falls well short of what is needed, if we are to maintain our numbers. Dr Howard offered a sobering projection of where business as usual will take us. Outside of the consulting room, it would seem we are no longer 'outside of time'.

There is a sense that, overcoming our desire to 'flock and forget', we are now collectively taking some action to meet the challenge of preserving our threatened species. Efforts are being made to improve 'outreach' programs, increase recruitment into training in the different centres, ensuring expectations on candidates remain realistic and not excessive, and to facilitate candidates progress without compromising standards. This year, The Sydney Institute for Psychoanalysis launched a one year, one evening a week, 'Psychodynamic Psychotherapy Course' for psychotherapist clinicians, intended to help deepen conceptual and theoretical understandings. It was fully subscribed for the first year, and will be run again next year. Our hope is that this and other local initiatives will eventually translate into applications for training.

I found Ahumada's article of particular interest in his analysis of the hostility towards psychoanalysis inherent in 'current sociocultural changes'. Ahumada characterizes these changes as a 'passage from the culture of the written word to one of action-images', which in his opinion constitutes 'the most drastic global experiment that the human species has willingly submitted to.' (Ahumada, 2013 p. 41). Such cultural shifts must be extremely difficult to 'read' accurately, but it does seem possible, at least in so-called 'Western culture', that we are entering an era where psychic reality is ever more relentlessly enacted and evacuated; where –K (Bion, 1962 p. 95) increasingly holds the field.

Ahumada further characterizes this shift in terms of the gap between modernity and post-modernity (Ahumada, 2013 p. 41). The tenets of the Enlightenment were a vital part of the intellectual tradition from which Freud's thinking grew. Today's psychoanalyst might, in turn, be described as born of the union between the Freudian revolution and the humanist-modernist development. But there is no reason why our intellectual and creative psychoanalytic tradition should remain in-step with the times. The essence of psychoanalysis is not a matter of fashion, and we can never become post-modernists; although of course 'post-modernists' might believe they can become, or indeed already are, psychoanalysts!

Inherent in the fabric of psychoanalytic thinking is belief in the presence of a 'truth', however difficult to apprehend, that lies beyond individual subjective interpretation. Perhaps it is possible for contradictories to exist side by side in the unconscious as Freud suggested, but if it is to remain meaningful, discourse about the unconscious, like discourse about anything, cannot ignore the law of non-contradiction (nothing can be both A and not-A). For the psychoanalyst interpreting the text can never be a matter of 'anything goes', and post-modern and psychoanalytic positions are not simply two different vertices from which we might view the world. A fundamental logical incompatibility remains, and in this sense no dialogue is possible (Goldblatt, 2006).

Ahumada suggests that current sociocultural changes 'will increasingly impinge, on the practice of psychoanalysis as we have known it', and may 'redefine the function of psychoanalysis' (Ahumada, 2013 p. 41), but as he also suggests, they do not alter the essence of what psychoanalysis is; they cannot impinge upon the noumenon (Symington, 2012).

Rustin and Stokoe cogently identify our collective need for our psychoanalytic 'institutions' to adapt to external realities if they are to survive. However, 'institutional' survival alone cannot ensure we maintain contact with a living 'psychoanalysis'. The challenge for psychoanalysts in Australia, and perhaps throughout the West, would seem to be whether we can adapt to a changing world without losing contact with our 'dreaming'; a greater catastrophe, I believe, than any loss of our socio-cultural profile.

Rigorous, if not ruthless, self-analysis will be an essential part of our process of adaptation, but as Ahumada also suggests, 'Grasping how culture has veered helps cushion disappointment and self-blame' (Ahumada, 2013 p. 42). If we are to adapt and survive, we will also have to accept and mourn external losses, and one of these would seem to be the loss entailed in the hostile shift in the socio-cultural climate. In the face of our diminishing profile, simply remaining self-critically and exclusively focused upon ourselves is only likely to lead to a melancholic attachment to better days, and a masochistic relation to the external world. We will need to remain realistic about that world, and in the face of hostility, need to have faith in an essence of something resilient within ourselves. This might be characterized in terms of our relationship with our 'dreaming'; our psychoanalytic 'truth'. Perhaps we can take a lesson from the sulphur-crested cockatoos, birds of the bush which have adapted to an urbanized environment and now thrive in the Sydney suburbs. I have no sense that they have lost anything of their essence in doing so. The cockatoos have not sacrificed their raucous and rumbustious selves. Probably it is these very self-assertive qualities that have ensured their survival; not only have they adapted to their new environment, but they have a way of insisting that the environment takes notice of, and accommodates to, them.

'Alone we are born/and die alone', wrote New Zealand poet, James K. Baxter (Baxter, 1948). Psychoanalysis would seem to be one human way in which we attempt, through contact with a shared psychic reality or 'truth', to transcend aloneness and outsideness, and deepen the meaning of our brief journey between birth and oblivion. If, as individuals we have found this path valuable, what we can do to make it attractive to others is perhaps rather limited. Probably the most important thing we really can do is to continue our search; our attempt to find and be ourselves. This should help us become less self-conscious, more assertive, more playful, and more adaptable.

Acknowledgement

For my outline sketch of the history of psychoanalysis in Australia I have relied in particular on Maria Teresa Hooke's 2010 address to the EPF, 'The tyranny of distance', and Frances Thomson-Salo's chapter: 'The Australian Psychoanalytical Society: the evolving relationship with the IPA. In 100 Years of the IPA'.

References

Ahumada, J.L. (2013). Minding the gap in changed times: a view from afar—Buenos Aires, Argentina. *Bulletin of the BPAS* 49(1):41–48.

Akhtar, S. (2007). The trauma of geographical dislocation: leaving, arriving, mourning, and becoming. In M.T.S. Hooke and S. Akhtar (Eds.). *The Geography of Meanings: Psychoanalytic Perspectives on Place, Space, Land, and Dislocation*. London: International Psychoanalysis Library.

Baxter, J.K. (1979). *High Country Weather*. In J.E. Weir (Ed.). *Collected Poems*. London: Oxford University Press. (Original work published 1948).

Bion, W. (1962). *Learning from Experience*. London: William Heinemann, Medical Books.

Damousi, J. (2005). *Freud in the Antipodes: a cultural history of psychoanalysis in Australia*. Sydney: UNSW Press.

Eliot, T.S. (1975). *Tradition and the Individual Talent*. In F. Kermode (Ed.). *Selected Prose of T.S. Eliot* (pp. 37–44). London: Faber & Faber. (Original work published 1919).

Goldblatt, M. (2006). *Can humanists talk to postmodernists?* ducts.org, Issue 17: Summer 2006. http://ducts.sundresspublications.com/06_06/html/reviews/goldblatt.html

Hooke, M.T.S. (2010). *The tyranny of distance. The early history of the Australian Psychoanalytical Society; a personal view*. Oral paper delivered to European Psychoanalytical Federation, London.

Hughes, R. (1988). *The Fatal Shore*. London: Pan Books.

Rustin, M. (2012). Reflections on the present condition of the British Psychoanalytical Society. *Bulletin of the BPAS* 48(2):31–35.

Stokoe P. (2012). Thoughts about the critical state of our society. *Bulletin of the BPAS* 48(4):30–33.

‘Think pig! Think!’: Beckett and Bion, *Waiting for Godot*

Both Samuel Beckett and Wilfred Bion possessed a certain genius for pithy aphoristic comments. To translate Beckett from the French:

> ‘When you are up to your neck in shit, there’s nothing for it but to sing.’

The image suggests a claustrophobic panic and paralysis; a shut-down of everything but the vital functions and the voice. Not much to sing about, perhaps.

Along similar lines, Bion spoke of the necessary willingness in analyst or patient to ‘make the best of a bad job’ (1979 p. 321).

Self-knowledge is implicit. If we are to make the best of our lives, or indeed to be free to sing, we are going to need to know something about the bad job—that is who we are and where we are.

At the end of 1933 Beckett, who was 27, entered into therapy with Bion, who was 36. Beckett would spend two years with Bion attending sessions three times a week.

When Beckett began the therapy, he had been in a bad way psychologically for some time, struggling with various symptoms including crippling anxiety. Then in 1933 his father, whom he had experienced as the supportive parental figure, died unexpectedly after two heart attacks. He was only 61. Beckett was present and recalled his father’s last words: ‘Fight fight fight. What a morning!’ (Letters p. 165). We immediately hear the resonance with Beckett's own voice and turn of phrase, as, for example, in the last words of his novel *The Unnamable*, 'I can't go on, I'll go on.'

After his father's death Beckett was walking in Dublin one day, and felt something like physical paralysis; he could not go on. He took himself off to his doctor friend Geoffrey Thompson who is said to have recommended 'psychoanalysis', and suggested the Tavistock Clinic in London. It doesn't seem that he specifically recommended Bion, who was just setting up in practice at the Tavistock. Bion wouldn't begin his formal psychoanalytic training until 1937 with John Rickman as his training analyst. Beckett was one of his very first therapy patients, and it seems rather remarkable that the man who would become the greatest playwright in English in the second half of the Twentieth Century, should have entered into therapy with the man destined to become the definitive psychoanalytic thinker of the same period.

What I will try and do is use *Waiting for Godot* to explore resonances, and to some extent a confluence, between Beckett's and Bion's thinking subsequent to their shared experience. Each found a similar, and in some respects congruent, vision of the human condition, which Beckett would realize in his creative writing, and Bion in the realm of psychoanalytic thinking.

Beckett would not write *Waiting for Godot* until after the Second World War, and it was first performed in 1953. Bion would not read his first psychoanalytic paper, 'The Imaginary Twin' until 1950. In 1933 then, we might say both men were still waiting…

Background literature

A great deal has already been written and conjectured about this encounter. Much of the literature to date focuses on the idea of mutual influence.

Bennett Simon in a 1988 paper in the International Journal of Psychoanalysis (IJP), 'The imaginary twins: the case of Beckett and Bion', has suggested that a kind of twinship and mutual influence existed between them. He speculates in particular on the influence he believes Bion may have experienced from Beckett, and goes so far as to suggest that Bion's depiction of his patient in 'The imaginary twin', is likely to be in part at least based on Beckett. Didier Anzieu (1989) in a subsequent paper suggests much of Beckett's subsequent work can be read as a working through of his unresolved experience with Bion. More recently Ian Miller in a book *Beckett and Bion*, offers support for Simon's conjectures, and the idea of mutual influence.

Bion suggested that when two personalities meet, an 'emotional storm' is created, and it is impossible that these two did not have an impact upon one another. Beckett's recently published letters offer some insights into Bion's impact upon him. But Bion, of course, left no direct public record of the experience with Beckett, and as Lois Oppenheim (2001), has pointed out in a later paper in the IJP, we have no direct evidence linking Bion's patient with Beckett, or to establish many of influences Simon and Anzieu suggest.

In order to understand the resonance between Bion's and Beckett's vision of the human condition, we need to look beyond the idea of mutual influence to the presence of a third. The third being that of an independent psychic reality of the human mind.

Simon also suggests the idea that Beckett was grappling 'artistically' with the same issues that Bion was grappling with 'theoretically and systematically' (Simon, p. 10). I think it is only through the perspective of the exploration of a third and independent reality from different vertices, that we can really make sense of the resonance. It also helps to understand the potentially profound and disturbing impact of Beckett's writings upon his audiences, and similarly the potentially profound and disturbing impact of Bion's formulations for psychoanalysts.

The play

Godot is a play in two acts, which take place over two successive days; the interval is the night between the days. The action of Act II in many ways mirrors that of Act I, with some important differences. It has been quipped that, *Waiting for Godot* is a play in which nothing happens… twice. I will consider just the first act.

The setting is a wasteland with a single leafless tree. Two tramps Vladimir and Estragon, or Didi and Gogo, as they call each other, are waiting for a Mr Godot, who never appears. The identity of Godot, in fact his very existence seems in question. Several other characters, Pozzo and Lucky, and a small boy do appear.

The play opens

> **Estragon:** Nothing to be done.
> **Vladimir:** I'm beginning to come round to that opinion. All my life I've tried to put it from me, saying, Vladimir, be reasonable, you haven't tried everything. And I resumed the struggle. (Turns toward **E**) So there you are again.
> **E** Am I?
> **V** I'm glad to see you back. I thought you were gone for ever.
> **E** Me too.
>
> (1954 p. 7)

Estragon's first words: 'Nothing to be done', refer to some difficulty with his boots and physical pain. Vladimir responds in a philosophical mode, and we are introduced to some undefined psychological problem suggesting emotional pain, rather than a simply physical one. A psychological difficulty is perhaps enacted by Vladimir in his ignoring Estragon as a human presence. Only after his musings does he really seem to notice Estragon and turn towards him.

Estragon responds with uncertainty "Am I?"

I think of Bion's injunction in 'Notes on memory and desire', 'The psychoanalyst should aim at achieving a state of mind so that at every session he feels he has not seen the patient before. If he feels he has he is treating the wrong patient' (p 19). Bion advises strenuously against trying to fill in the gaps in our memory. 'The only point of importance in the session is the unknown' (p. 17). Any conscious attempt to retrieve memories, or to further desires, will, Bion suggests, disrupt the possibility that 'Out of the darkness and formlessness something evolves' (p. 18).

Bion emphasizes the necessary capacity to tolerate uncertainty and the frustration of uncertainty, if mental growth is to occur. He formulates this in his injunction to eschew memory, desire, understanding; in his idea of the oscillation between PS and D, and his insistence on the need to wait for a new D, that is for a new meaning, to emerge through the apprehension of the selected fact. Quoting Keats's concept of 'negative capability'; the task is to tolerate 'uncertainties, mysteries, doubts, without any irritable reaching after fact and reason' (1970 p. 125). We have probably heard and read these ideas so many times we may well have become deaf to just how radical they are. Whether or not it was Bion's intention they tend to be subversive of our institutionalized orthodoxies.

The opening of *Godot* captures such a sense of the uncertain and unknown.

This opening dialog also seems to offer a representation of unconscious processes which might be present at the beginning of a psychoanalytic session. The patient might be anxious that the analyst has disappeared between sessions, possibly destroyed by the patient's own aggression.

'Oh, there you are' says the analyst to the patient, or the patient to the analyst. 'Am I?' questions the patient, or indeed the analyst. After all, the patient at least probably wouldn't be there at all, if he knew enough about where he was and who he was. Maybe the same may sometimes be true for the analyst.

Aggression doesn't take long to appear. Vladimir goes on to enquire of Estragon where he spent the night:

> **V** May one inquire where His Highness spent the night?
> **E** In a ditch.
> **V** A ditch! Where?
> **E** Over there.
> **V** And they didn't beat you?
> **E** Beat me? Certainly, they beat me.
> **V** The same lot as usual?
> **E** The same? I don't know.
>
> (1954 p. 7)

A persecutory world is evoked, in an experience like a recurring nightmare. The problems of persecution, and what we might call a schizoid withdrawal in response to anxiety about the survival of the other, are explicit at the outset. Does this uncertainty about the survival of the object, 'I thought you were gone forever', underlie Vladimir's reluctance to turn towards Estragon, his preference, at least initially for a philosophical discourse with himself?

A few minutes further into the play and the enigmatic Mr Godot is invoked for the first time:

> **E** Charming spot. Inspiring prospects. Let's go.
> **V** We can't.
> **E** Why not?

V We're waiting for Godot.

In response to a question as to whether Godot represented God, Beckett once commented, '…if by Godot I had meant God I would have said God and not Godot… ' (Knowlson, p. 412). He was often irritated by this sort of 'reaching after fact and reason'.

Nevertheless, Godot does seem to represent, for Vladimir at least, a possible solution: 'We're saved!' (1954 p. 47). Godot seems to stand for something like the omnipotence of a magic solution; in this form we conclude fairly early on that he isn't going to turn up. Or perhaps he might stand for the psychoanalytic object as Bion formulates it; present, but in essence unknowable.

Apparently, they are to wait by the tree. The tree is a symbol of life but where are the leaves? There are none:

E Where are the leaves?
V It must be dead.
E No more weeping.
V Or perhaps it's not the season.

Adds Vladimir, allowing an uncertainty which leaves open a possibility the tree is not dead. No hope as such is expressed, but there is a suggestion of faith; faith that the transformation of the seasons remains a possibility.

They are to wait; waiting for new life, is at the heart of the psychoanalytic endeavour. No one has explored this dimension as fully as Bion.

Uncertainty and frustration are everywhere in *Godot*. Vladimir and Estragon are forced to live with what they cannot tolerate; they are continually seeking to evade both. As Bion suggests 'Any emotional experience that is felt to be painful may initiate an attempt either to evade or modify the pain according to the capacity of the personality to tolerate frustration' (1962 p.48). Complete evasion leads to knowledge that is felt to be free from pain, but this blocks and restricts emotional growth.

In *Learning from experience* Bion suggests two relatively distinct modes of thinking. First, the emergence of coherent meaning through the apprehension of the 'selected fact', and second the use of understandings and intuitions generated in this way to build theoretical structures; these he calls 'scientific deductive systems'. To be of use such a system must be internally consistent, and respect laws of logic and deductive reasoning.

However, Bion (1993) also comments astutely that any attempt to impose a 'scientific deductive system' appropriate to the inanimate world, on human experience, has weaknesses close to that of psychotic thinking (1962 p. 14). Such a system, if imposed on human experience, leads to links which, may be 'logical, almost mathematical, but never emotional reasonable' (p. 109). We might consider contemporary biological psychiatry in this regard.

Interestingly Bion (1993) also suggests where the capacity to tolerate frustration is absent, an appreciation of the dimensions of space and time cannot evolve (p. 136).

We might consider suicide as the ultimate evasion of psychic pain and reality, and the question of suicide soon appears, in a kind of burlesque tragicomic scene (1954 p. 12). Vladimir and Estragon contemplate hanging themselves from a tree that seems to be dead. The excitement of the sexual dimension of hanging, **V** "It'd give us an erection" (ibid. p. 12), suggests an escape from deadness, but it also will be a dead end; a perversion.

Estragon's idea: 'How about hanging ourselves' is a delusional and psychotic solution. As such it stands as a parody of the selected fact experience.

The discussion about who should hang first framed in terms of who is heaviest does have an intact logic which we can follow should we wish to do so, but any emotional reality has been obliterated. This is the logic appropriate to the inanimate world and is misplaced, leading only to links 'perverse, cruel, and sterile' (Bion, 1993 p. 109). This particular 'logical deductive system' leads nowhere.

In the end nothing happens; neither Vladimir nor Estragon, it seems, really want to die. 'Don't let's do anything. It's safer' says Estragon, with a step back towards sanity. There is also the wonderful subtle hypocrisy in Estragon's suggestion that he wouldn't want Vladimir to be left alone, should he successfully hang himself and Vladimir fail. 'You're my only hope' (1954 p. 12).

Mandrakes (ibid. p. 12) are a sedative and analgesic. They are also said to grow beneath the gallows where murderers are hung, and shriek horribly if dug up. Anyone who hears the shriek apparently will also die.

When the patient suicides he is enacting an intrapsychic suicide that has already occurred. In this complex dialogue, Beckett brilliantly links unbearable pain, the attempt to deaden it in the service of survival, and the intrapsychic suicide that follows; the destruction that ensues from the evasion of pain.

The first act becomes electrifying when Pozzo and Lucky appear, especially when Lucky embarks on his 'think'. The eruption of a disturbing state of mind may be felt by the audience.

If played well, there is awe at the power of the performance. It can feel like an electric current that goes straight in. Perhaps the experience reflects the impact of what Bion calls the Beta Screen, when Alpha Function is reversed, and the contact barrier separating conscious and unconscious mind has momentarily broken down. Perhaps the experience was one of contact with 'O'. Whatever the explanatory value of such ideas, I believe that correctly interpreted and performed Beckett's dramatic works possess an inherent capacity to impact upon us, because they resonate at such a fundamental level of shared psychic reality.

A psychic catastrophe, as Bion has called it, is being evoked. We are in the presence of it, and we are invited to live it vicariously as audience. Just in case we haven't quite registered the catastrophe, and to some extent diversion is possible, because the action and dialog are at times so very funny... so just in case we haven't quite registered this catastrophe, Beckett brings on stage Pozzo and Lucky. For me they are among the great characters of drama.

The pompous Pozzo claims to be a personage of significance, but is traversing what he claims is his land, on foot, accompanied by his carrier Lucky. Pozzo controls Lucky by means of a long heavy rope around his neck, a whip which he cracks menacingly, and barked commands. The relationship seems purely sadomasochistic. As we know, you can't have one without the other. The mutual dependency is complete, represented by the heavy rope that links. (1954 p. 15)

A work of art is, I think, successful to the extent that the transformation offered allows us to enter into lived experience; to the extent the artist is able to evoke experience that is shared.

With Pozzo and Lucky, it seems we are suddenly introduced to a different vertex on the situation of the play. As if exploring at a deeper level within the twin characters of Vladimir and Estragon; by inference of everyman and everywoman, and of course ourselves.

Pozzo and Lucky are like figures from the engine room of the psyche; Pozzo evokes for me the idea of a bloated and cruel superego figure who has swallowed all life, all id perhaps, into a purely destructive organization. Lucky evokes the idea of a depleted ego, stripped of will and feeling, like the tree, maybe a weeping willow without leaves; although at one point the tramps notice that Lucky is weeping briefly.

Pozzo offers to have Lucky dance or think. Vladimir questions in astonishment: 'He thinks?'

The dance is a pathetic one in the true sense of the word. (1954 p. 27)

The 'think' follows. 'He can't think without his hat' explains Pozzo. So, Vladimir puts the necessary hat on Lucky's head, cautiously as not long before Lucky had given Estragon a swift kick in the shin.

The 'think' begins:

Lucky: 'Given the existence as uttered forth in the public works of Puncher and Wattmann of a personal God quaquaquaqua…'

And escalates in speed towards a kind of manic crescendo of associations. It is a parody of thinking; here words seem to be being used like missiles to evacuate any possibility of a creative thinking-feeling experience. (ibid. p. 29)

It ends when Pozzo yells 'His hat!' Vladimir removes Lucky's hat and Lucky falls silent, and then falls down. The relief when it is over is palpable.

In Bion's language we might say the mental contents appear to have exploded their container. The fragments that explode out are like 'bizarre objects'.

What makes this bearable, indeed fascinating, is Beckett's genius of expression, in the context of the separation offered by the theatre. These create a balance where we are both vicariously drawn in but can remain sufficiently outside; we are invited into a space where some reverie is possible, at least after the performance.

It has been remarked that Bion's writing style encourages the frame of mind he describes as receptive to the selected fact; it becomes necessary to read and relinquish any determination to understand; to allow oneself to go with the incoherence and just wait for something to emerge.

It is striking how Beckett leaves us with very little choice but to approach his plays, and also his prose, in a similar way; to find a reverie where meaning may, or indeed may not, emerge. Any attempt to impose a singular type of explanation founders, because any certainty is continuously undercut.

Concluding comments

I want to take issue with an idea in Ian Miller's (2013) recent and very interesting book on Beckett and Bion. This is his locating both men in the post-modern tradition. This is a commonplace view of Beckett. Of course, we can see what Miller is getting at, in that the texts of both authors undercut orthodoxies and emphasize the unknown. In contrast Anthony Cronin, has called his, I would say rather brilliant, biography of Beckett *The last modernist*, and this seems to be more on track (1996).

Perhaps a great writer can be a post-modernist, but I doubt it will do for a psychoanalyst. The essence of psychoanalytic work, as I think Bion suggests, is work towards truth and authenticity. Accepting the impossibility of ever grasping the Truth, or the essence of being, is not the same thing as believing that all interpretations of the text are of equal value, or all expressions of the self equally valid. Bion the most radical of psychoanalytic thinkers, was a relativist only in a relative sense.

Bion spoke of the 'spontaneous bleakness' of the truth (Symington, J and N., 1996 p. 80). An accurate interpretation that can be heard, tends to have a sobering effect. Sobering because such an interpretation always undercuts our self-inflation.

Bleakness there is aplenty in *Godot*. I read in the play a critique of overvalued ideas of all sorts and ultimately of the idea, also an inflated one, that all thoughts and experience are of equal status (the shit perhaps that is up to the neck). One of the changes that takes place between Act I and Act II, to the astonishment of both Vladimir and Estragon, is that the tree sprouts a few leaves. The tree begins to sing. New Zealand poet Michael Harlow has described Beckett as the poet of dark hope. This is apt, but I think the poet of dark faith may capture it more truly.

Bion and Beckett each offer views from particular and personal vertices, but as I've suggested the power inherent in their respective visions and the resonance between them, suggests that each offers a transformation that accurately captures elements of the independent reality of the human condition.

We know something of the influence of Bion on Beckett from Beckett's letters. Ian Miller (2013) seems right in concluding that Beckett left, probably fled, his therapy with Bion prematurely, and he is also right in suggesting that Beckett nevertheless took a lot from Bion. There is much to suggest that the therapy got Beckett writing again, and probably gave him something to write about. He began his novel *Murphy* towards the end of the therapy. After the interruption and disruption of WWII, Beckett entered a period of great creativity, during which he wrote his famous trilogy of novels, and *Godot* contemporaneously.

There is much in all of these texts suggesting that he continued to work through elements of the experience with Bion. My intuition, for what it is worth, is that the leaves that appear on the tree are, amongst other things, a debt of gratitude to Bion. As a therapist Bion did seem to help bring new creative life to Beckett, to help him get writing and singing again; not completely buried in the shit.

Beckett had a very good relationship with his father, and a terrible one with his mother. Of course, things are never quite so simple, but it probably links to the emergence of a transference with Bion that Beckett was able to use in a helpful, if limited, way. The young boy in Godot, who appears at the end of each act also seems to link to hope. The figures of a man and boy, often walking hand in hand, is a recurring motif in Beckett's work. Beckett's prose piece *Worstward Ho* seems to capture something inherent in the nature of psychoanalytic work, and perhaps has a resonance with Beckett's experience with Bion:

> 'Ever tried. Ever failed. No matter. Try again. Fail again. Fail better.'

I'll finish with a poem of my own, submitted to and published by the Irish literary magazine *Crannog*, number 39.

Encounter: Beckett/Bion

Imagination
Sentience
journeying
to this moment
now

Dead
Sentence
as in darkness
to wait
at cross-roads

a bleak dawn
to crack the sky
four chalk roads
a broken cairn

Imagine

Turn
the four directions
earth emptied
of travellers
unless—
can it be?

a very long
long way away
man and boy
hand in hand
walking

they pass beyond
a final
distant hill
I cannot be sure
to have seen
yet
see them still

References

Anzieu, D. (1989). Beckett and Bion. *International Review Psychoanalysis* 16:163–169.

Beckett, S. (1954). *Waiting for Godot*. New York: Grove Press.

Bion, W R. (1993). *Second Thoughts*, London: Karnac. (Original works published 1950 & 1959).

——— (1994). *Learning from Experience*. London: Jason Aronson. (Original work published 1962).

——— (1969). Notes on memory and desire. First published in Spanish by *Revista de Psicoanalisis*. 26(3): 679–681.

——— (1984). *Attention and Interpretation*. London: Karnac. (Original work published 1970).

——— (1979). Making the best of a bad job. In: Bion (1994) *Clinical Seminars,* London: Karnac.

Cronin, A. (1996). *The Last Modernist*. London: Harper Collins.

Fehsenfeld, M.D. & Overbeck, L.M. (Eds.). (2009). *The Letters of Samuel Beckett 1929–1940*. Cambridge: Cambridge University Press.

Knowlson, J. (1996). *Damned to Fame: The Life of Samuel Beckett*. London: Bloomsbury.

Miller, I., & Souter, K. (2013). *Beckett and Bion*. London: Karnac.

Oppenheim, L. (2001). A preoccupation with object-representation: The Beckett-Bion case revisited. *International Journal of Psychoanalysis*. 82(4):767–784.

Simon, B. (1988). The imaginary twins: the case of Beckett and Bion. *International Review Psychoanalysis* 15:331–352.

Symington, J. & Symington, N. (1996). *The Clinical Thinking of Wilfred Bion*. London: Routledge.

Mind over matter?
I: Philosophical aspects of the mind-brain problem

Published in *The Australian and New Zealand Journal of Psychiatry* 2001, 35:481–487

'Man can embody truth but he cannot know it.'

—W.B. Yeats

This paper is concerned with the nature of the relationship between 'mental' mind phenomena and 'material' brain phenomena; in other words, the 'mind-brain' or 'mind-body' problem. Following an examination of the general nature of the problem, it establishes two working propositions which are employed in the attempt to conceptualize the mind in its relationship to the brain

Historical Background

A brief note on some of the influential ideas may help place the contemporary situation in perspective.

The French philosopher Rene Descartes (1596–1650) is known for his lucid formulation of 'mind' or 'soul' as something distinct from body, and of which we have indubitable knowledge (see Anscombe E and Geach P.T., 1970). Consequently, he is often condemned for 'creating' the mind-body problem. Gilbert Ryle (1949) has suggested Descartes's formulation contributed to the growth of a myth, which over time has become a kind of official doctrine and dogma in Western Society; the dogma of 'the ghost in the machine'. Although Descartes gave clearer form to the dualist conception of mind as distinct from matter, dualist systems of thought were influential before Descartes and can be traced at least as far back as the ancient Greeks.

Descartes considered mind or soul and body to be ontologically distinct, that is two things of different essential natures; yet his observation revealed that they seemed to exert effects upon one another. How could two things fundamentally different in nature act upon each other? Descartes postulated that the pineal gland was the seat of mind-body interactions which he conceived of as being mediated by the 'animal spirits', but beyond that was unable to specify the mechanism by which such interaction might take place (Hatfield G., 1992).

Contemporary commentators, in highlighting the shortcomings of Descartes's dualism, often overlook the elegance and clarity of his central formulation in the Meditations: I think therefore I am. Descartes, beginning from a position of epistemological scepticism, apprehended reasons to doubt all commonly accepted forms of knowledge, leaving only the apparently indubitable reality of his own consciousness as a given. There may be grounds to doubt the existence of everything, he reasoned, but the very act of doubting implies at least the existence of one's own mind. This much cannot be doubted: 'I am, I exist; that is certain'. Descartes then took this acquaintance with one's own mind as the rational starting point for establishing a system of ontology. In his 6th Meditation (Anscombe E, Geach P.T. eds, 1970 pp. 109–124), Descartes apprehended that mental events, especially in the realm of understanding or intellect, appeared to constitute an area of discourse distinct from physical bodily events; each area of discourse possessing different explanatory parameters. In Bertrand

Russell's words '"I think, therefore I am" makes mind more certain than matter, and my mind (for me) more certain than the minds of others' and, 'The decision … to regard thoughts rather than external objects as the prime empirical certainties was very important, and had a profound effect on all subsequent philosophy.' (Russell, B ,1984 pp. 542–551)

Since Descartes, formulations and attempted solutions to the mind-body problem have been many and varied, but can be broadly divided into 'dualist', which assert the existence of two sorts of 'stuff' (substances, processes, being) which co-exist, and 'monist', which assert the existence of only one fundamental 'stuff', which is the basis of all observable phenomena.

Dualist explanations may be further subdivided into interactionist, such as Descartes's, and non-interactionist. The apparently implausible theory of 'psychophysical parallelism', as found in the philosophy of Leibniz (1646–1716), provides an example of a non-interactionist dualist theory. Leibniz postulated that there are two kinds of existence, body and mind, which parallel each other but are completely separate and do not interact. Thus, their apparent interaction is but an illusion; the consequence of a preordained and on-going harmony, established originally by God (Woolhouse and Francks eds, 1998).

A dualist theory of historical importance, and continuing influence within psychiatry, is epiphenomenalism. In philosophical terms an epiphenomenon is a by-product which exerts no causal effect. Epiphenomenalism proposes that mind is a dependent and passive secondary phenomenon caused by the activity of the brain. It is essentially non-interactionist, proposing a one-way causality from brain to mind. Such a view constitutes a rigidly deterministic formulation of mind, and its ascendance was contributed to by Darwin's elucidation of deterministic principles in biology. The concept of soul, so intrinsic to much dualist thought, was threatened, and for many had been routed, by Darwin's evolutionary theory. Epiphenomenalism found particular favour with

Darwin's 'disciple' Thomas Henry Huxley, who seems to have conceived of man as a kind of biological automaton (Huxley 1897).

Monist solutions fall broadly into three categories: idealist solutions which assert that the 'stuff' of the universe is mind and its contents; materialist solutions which assert that the 'stuff' of the universe is matter and its properties; and attempts to formulate mind and matter as, in essence, identical, or as different aspects of a unity.

The name most closely associated with the idealist option is Bishop Berkeley (1685–1753). Russell (1984) summarizes Berkeley's position as a denial of the existence of matter, maintaining that material objects only exist through being perceived. Thus, physical bodies are regarded as not existing as such; it is only the ideas of bodies that exist in minds. Elsewhere, Russell (1967) acknowledges that because no absolute proof of the independent existence of matter seems possible, idealist arguments are difficult to refute decisively. He nevertheless attempts a commonsense refutation of Berkeley's position. He points to the counterintuitive nature of pure idealist theories and their lack of explanatory economy as good reasons not to embrace them. Although idealist perspectives have had great influence within philosophy, they have fared less well in the face of the growth of empiricism in science, and the practical and pragmatic successes that have flowed from the industrial and technological revolutions.

It would probably be fair to say that 'materialism' (as a philosophical/intellectual perspective) became the major influence in the West in the twentieth century, with attempted materialist solutions to the mind-body problem asserting the primacy of matter. At the extreme the doctrine of materialism denies the existence of mind. Such an assertion is, probably for most of us, difficult to accept, and might be considered demonstrably false, in that something we call 'mind' is apprehended through introspection and seems to require explanation. A less extreme materialism might regard mind as an epiphenomenon, or as something not remarkably different from the brain or body, and therefore reducible to description in terms of physical parameters.

In more recent times, through the perspectives provided by modern physics, matter has begun to look less 'substantial' than it once did, and materialist perspectives have developed into physicalist perspectives which look towards the physical universe as a whole, that is matter and the physical forces and properties associated with matter, in the attempt to conceptualize the mind.

The increase in the influence of materialist/physicalist intellectual perspectives was linked with the rise of empirical methods in the physical sciences, and positivism in philosophy. In psychology, the outcome of the tendency to ignore the mind was methodological behaviourism. The term behaviourism may be applied to a scientific method; 'methodological behaviourism', or to a philosophical perspective; 'logical behaviourism'. The early proponent of behaviourism as an investigative methodology in psychology, B. F. Skinner, in his book Science and human behaviour (p. 12), exhorts his reader to forget about mental phenomena, which seem to be regarded as irrelevant. He writes that in certain situations 'the mind and the ideas, together with their special characteristics, are being invented on the spot to provide spurious explanations. A science of behaviour can hope to gain very little from so cavalier a practice. Since mental or psychic events are asserted to lack the dimensions of physical science, we have an additional reason for rejecting them.'

In *The concept of mind* (p. 5) the influential philosopher Gilbert Ryle attempted to undermine the supposed dogma of the 'ghost in the machine', by arguing a form of 'logical behaviourism'. Ryle suggests '...the styles and procedures of people's activities are the way their minds work and are not merely imperfect reflections of the postulated secret processes which were supposed to be the workings of minds'. Ryle also attempts to invalidate Descartes's concept of privileged access to one's own mind by arguing that self-knowledge and knowledge about others are on a parity: 'The sorts of things that I can find out about myself are the same as the sorts of things that I can find out about other people, and the methods of finding them out are much the same.' While there is much commonsense here and, as Ryle argues, it seems probable that we obtain our understanding of the way others' minds work from their behaviour, it is hard to see how Ryle's arguments can do justice to the reality and dimensions of subjective mental experience. An observer's understanding of a person's behaviour can never constitute a full knowledge of that person's mind; there always remains an inaccessible and 'ghostly' aspect in the experience of another. In order to fully know the nature of another's experience of physical pain, I would have to feel his or her pain; presumably not a possibility (see below) See also Wallace (1988) for a critique of some aspects of Ryle's logic from within a psychiatric framework.

With the development of increasingly sophisticated techniques for direct brain investigation in the second half of the 20th century and 21st century, the main focus for scientific investigation of mental states has shifted from the empirical observation of human behaviour, to the empirical observation of the brain. Research over the course of the last century has provided increasing evidence for the linkage between mental events and physical brain events. Contemporary monist materialist views propose an identity between mental states and states of the material brain.

Today most of us would probably accept the proposition that the existence of the mind is in some way contingent upon the existence and function of the material brain. We would regard the function of the mind as intimately and probably inextricably linked with the function of the brain, and we would not expect a mind in the absence of a functioning brain.

The contemporary situation

If mental events are contingent upon brain events in this kind of way, does that mean they are reducible to brain events? Many scientists and philosophers hold such a view, and within psychiatry it seems a commonplace assumption. There can be no doubt as to the influence of reductionist materialist/physicalist perspectives, and the dominant view in the West in the latter half of the twentieth century would seem to be a materialist 'identity theory' which posits that mental events are in fact brain events, and may be fully explained as brain events, thus the title of Daniel Dennett's book championing this position: *Consciousness explained* (1993).

There have, however, always been voices arguing the impossibility of a reductionist materialist understanding of mind. In 1960 the biologist Seymour Kety wrote in *Science* (1960):

> There remains one biological phenomenon, more central to psychiatry than to other fields, for which there is no valid physiochemical model and (or so it seems to me) little likelihood of developing one; this is the phenomenon of consciousness—the complex of present sensations and the memory of past experience which we call mind.

He goes on to suggest that, 'one can acknowledge the existence of consciousness and of matter and energy without insisting that one must be reduced to the other.'

Similarly, the philosopher John Searle, in his 1992 book *The rediscovery of the mind*, identifies the tendency in materialist doctrines 'to deny the existence of any irreducible mental phenomena in the world'. Searle asks, 'Now why are they (the reductionists) so anxious to deny the existence of irreducible intrinsic mental phenomena? Why don't they just concede that these properties are ordinary higher-level biological properties of neurophysiological systems such as human brains?' Searle argues the need to accept the 'obvious facts about our own experiences—for example, that we are all conscious and that our conscious states have quite specific *irreducible* phenomenological properties', is as necessary as the need to accept the 'obvious facts of physics.'

Searle goes on to argue that the mistake is to view the irreducibility of mental phenomena and the contingency of mind upon brain as incompatible realities which therefore imply a form of dualism. Searle asserts the irreducibility of mental events to physical events, but rejects dualism.

David Chalmers is another contemporary philosopher unimpressed by attempts to formulate a reductive materialist solution, but he is also unimpressed by Searle's idea that the phenomenon of consciousness is an instance of an ordinary higher level biological property, essentially similar to other higher level biological properties. Chalmers (1996) points out that the phenomena of consciousness differ from all other phenomena in that: 'Our grounds for belief in consciousness derive solely from our own experience of it.' Chalmers argues that consciousness is not logically entailed by the physical facts of the functioning human brain; that is consciousness is not 'logically supervenient' upon these facts:

> From all the low-level facts about physical configurations and causation, we can in principle derive all sorts of high-level facts about macroscopic systems, their organization, and the causation among them. One could determine all the facts about biological function, and about human behaviour and the brain mechanisms by which it is caused. But nothing in this vast causal story would lead one who had not experienced it directly to believe that there should be any *consciousness.*

Chalmers' argument here seems analogous to the argument entailed in the 'problem of other minds'; that is the problem of how we can ever know that someone else has a mind. An observer may infer from a person's behaviour and what he says about himself that the person is conscious, but it is not something of which the observer can have certain knowledge, nor confirmation by direct experience of the phenomena of that consciousness; it is an inductive inference rather than a logical necessity. Similarly, an observer may monitor the activity of a brain, and infer that the brain possessed consciousness, but can have no direct knowledge of this consciousness. The observations about a brain which form the basis for inference do not logically entail the existence of consciousness. Acquaintance with the existence of consciousness comes through one's own experience.

Many scientists and some philosophers, such as Dennett (1993), have asserted either that the 'mind-brain problem' has disappeared, or will eventually disappear, in the face of the growth of scientific knowledge about the functioning of the brain; that the burgeoning knowledge, consequent upon advances in investigative neuroscience, has finally proved that the human mind and brain are indeed one and the same thing.

Despite the evidence for the existence of a close correlation or 'identity' between brain events and mental events, and despite the fact that this evidence has shaped the way the mind-brain 'relationship' is conceptualized, there remains no consensus as to the correct understanding of the nature of this 'relationship'. It is, I think, probably mistaken to believe that growth in scientific knowledge can lead to such an understanding. That is to say that the essence of the problem remains a matter of metaphysics rather than physics.

The problem

The assumption that the mind-brain problem will eventually be solved by science, arises from a failure to recognize the nature of the problem. We already have sufficient grounds to assume, as a best hypothesis, that mental events and brain events constitute a fundamental unity; that there is at least an 'identity' of correlation between specific brain events or states and specific mental events or states. Ever since evidence for the link between mental and brain events has been available, some kind of identity theory has seemed the most reasonable working hypothesis. The details of a sophisticated contemporary scanning study linking mental activity and brain physiology reveal nothing essentially different, in relation to the mind-brain question, from say, Wilder Penfield's classic studies of cortical stimulation carried out more than 70 years ago (1975). Both studies provide data of the same explanatory order. Further scientific research is likely to reveal increasingly fine grain data about the mind-brain relationship, but it cannot be expected to yield data of a new explanatory order. Substantial evidence already exists for the mind-brain correlation that would be predicted by some form of 'identity' theory, and it seems a reasonable assumption that further research will provide consistent data.

The problem that science probably cannot reach, is how to give a satisfactory explanation of mental experience, or the phenomenology of consciousness, in terms of the brain. There does not seem to be a way. Any attempt at explanation inevitably ends up leaving out the mind.

The difficulty may be stated something like this: even if it were possible with sufficiently sophisticated scientific instruments to observe and measure all the neurophysiological correlates of a specific mental event, for example feeling a pain in the finger, this cannot communicate the essential subjective experience of the pain to the observer. An independent observer of these brain processes does not have a painful experience in his finger; he sees the various manifestations of neurophysiological processes. Even if he is aware that these manifestations equate with 'feeling a pain in the finger', he has no direct access to the subjective experience of the experimental subject, only indirect access, by inference, or from the subject's communications, about the experience. Any empathic identification with the pain experience on the observer's part remains just that, not the thing in itself. There is, it would appear, no way to get the essence of a subjective mental experience by observing a brain; this essence remains personal, and 'ghostly'.

An hypothetical example (slightly modified) taken from Chalmers' book *The conscious mind* (1996), adapted from Jackson (1982), may help to illustrate this. Imagine we live in an age of completed neuroscience, and know everything there is to know about physical processes in our brains. Mary has been bought up wearing spectacles which screen out colour, so she can see only black, white and grey. She has never taken them off and has never seen any colour. Mary is nevertheless very well educated as a neuroscientist specializing in the neurophysiology of colour vision. 'She knows everything there is to know about the neural processes involved in visual information processing, about the physics of optical processes, and about the physical makeup of objects in the environment', but she has never seen any colour. No amount of reasoning from the physical facts that are known to her can lead her to know what the experience of seeing in colour is like, for example 'she does not know what it is like to see red'. 'It follows that the facts about the subjective experience of colour vision are not entailed by the physical facts. If they were, Mary could in principle come to know what it is like to see red on the basis of her knowledge of the physical facts. But she cannot.'

In Chalmers' (1996) terminology, the mind and experience are 'naturally supervenient', but not 'logically supervenient', upon brain activity. Natural supervenience reflects the contingency of mind upon brain; that in all probability the mind cannot exist without the brain. Nevertheless, experience or mind is not logically supervenient, in that a full knowledge of brain events cannot lead to a full knowledge of the subjective experience of the mind that accompanies the brain. Or again, Chalmers comments, 'Whether or not consciousness *is* a biochemical structure, that is not what "consciousness" *means*.'

In Levine's terminology (1983) there is always an 'explanatory gap' between physical explanations of brain processes and the nature of experience in the mind. The subjective quality or 'feel' of experiences, referred to by philosophers as 'qualia', has a non-reductive aspect. Another way of putting this is that even if we assume our conscious mind is our experience of the activity of our brain, and even if we adopt a theory of the unity or identity of mind and brain, we do not and cannot, experience mind and body/brain as identical.

Thus, the problem that confronts us can be stated in terms of two propositions (constituting a 'double aspect theory') as follows:

The faculty of mind is contingent upon the functioning human brain; in this sense mind and brain constitute two aspects of a unity. At a fundamental level there appears to be an 'identity' between specific mental states and specific brain states upon which they are contingent.

Any attempt to explain the subjective essence of a mental state or process in terms of a brain state or process must inevitably fail as it leaves out the 'mind' that we seek to explain. Discourse about mental states is not reducible to discourse about brain states, and therefore brain states and mind states are not identical. (If *x* is identical to *y* then any property of *x* is also a property of *y*, and vice versa. Subjective mental events and objective brain events have distinct and differing properties.)

Both these statements can, I believe, be reasonably judged to be true: 1) on the basis that it best fits the available scientific data; 2) on the basis that it is a self-evident truth. However, taken together they are difficult to reconcile; they result at best in a paradox, at worst in logical incompatibility. On the one hand we 'know' that mind and brain in some fundamental way constitute unity, or exist in an 'identity'; on the other hand, our experience of our own mind cannot be reduced to description of brain processes and nor can the essence of mental experience be constructed out of knowledge of brain processes. How these non-identical constructs can be an 'identity' remains mysterious.

Whatever the logical difficulty in reconciling these two statements, it is no greater than the logical difficulty presented by other formulations of, or 'solutions' to, the mind-brain problem. As Wallace (1988) comments, 'At the current level of psychological, biological, and philosophical sophistication any approach to the mind-body problem is scandalous; none avoids logical and empirical pitfalls.' The question continues to preoccupy philosophers precisely because no satisfactory solution has been formulated. All attempted solutions to date suffer a 'fatal' flaw of incompleteness or internal contradiction, and the proposed formulation fares no worse in this regard. Any greater plausibility of the proposed formulation over alternatives rests solely on whether one judges the 'commonsense' validity of the propositions to be sufficiently compelling.

If the arguments put forward here are accepted, then we are left with a mystery at the heart of the mind-brain relationship; we simply cannot imaginatively grasp how mind comes about as a consequence of certain arrangements and activities of matter, but we know that it does. Furthermore, it seems unlikely that further scientific research, upon either brain or mind, can help us. If we take Searle's (1994) position then, despite the conceptual difficulties, we know the answer to our problem is that mind is a property of brain, and in principle this need be no more mysterious than the fact that liquidity is a property of water under certain conditions. Chalmers (1996), in contrast, believes that the situation is much more mysterious indeed, and argues persuasively that consciousness is a property that stands in an altogether different relationship to the brain than liquidity does to water.

Even if we wish to avoid a dualist view, we seem to be stuck phenomenologically with a sense of duality; we simply experience mind and body as distinct. There is a mystery at the heart of the mind-brain 'relationship', which it seems impossible for the mind to grasp, just as it appears to be beyond the capacity of the human mind, at least in its current state of development, to imaginatively grasp the concept of infinity. Regarding the problem as amenable to solution by the means of science appears to have more to do with wish than reality.

Commentators in psychiatry often contend that the 'Cartesian' distinction or 'split' between mind and body/brain is an artificial dichotomy and an imposition upon the unity that constitutes reality and exhort us to transcend this artificial distinction in our thinking. While it may be necessary to strive to transcend this dichotomy whenever it threatens to limit clinical thinking, it does not follow that 'dualist' thinking is problematic in principle, and therefore something to be dispensed with. In any case this is hardly possible. As has been argued, in order to think about the mind and its activity we need to have a concept of mind, and this inevitably involves distinguishing mind from either body or brain.

Our experience of duality would seem to be an unavoidable consequence of the emergence of a self aware and self reflecting mind. I suggest that one cannot have a mind, at least not a 'modern' mind without it, and that if we wished to do away with this sense of duality, we would have to be willing to forego the capacity for thoughtful self-awareness that constitutes our mind. For all the criticism that has been levelled at Descartes, he was, in his willingness to take the mind seriously, essentially a modern thinker.

By this view the human 'mind', in a collective historical sense, is also a developing function, and probably has different capacities today than it did, say, before Descartes's time. This being so, the possibility cannot be excluded that, in its collective function, the human mind could yet evolve to the point of possessing the capacity to imaginatively grasp how it emerges from matter.

References

Brown, L. (Ed.) (1993). *The New Shorter Oxford English Dictionary*. Oxford: Clarendon Press.

Chalmers, D.J. (1996). *The Conscious Mind: In Search of a Fundamental Theory*. Oxford: Oxford University Press.

Dennett, D.C. (1993). *Consciousness Explained.* London: Penguin.

Descartes R. (1970). Meditations on first philosophy. In E. Anscombe & P.T. Geach (Eds.) *Descartes's Philosophical Writings* (pp. 109–124). Sunbury-on-Thames: Thomas Nelson.

Hatfield, G. (1992). Descartes's physiology and its relation to his psychology. In J. Cottingham (Ed.). *The Cambridge Companion to Descartes* (pp. 335–370). Cambridge: Cambridge University Press.

Huxley, T.H. (1897). *Method and Results: Essays* (pp. 199–250). New York: D Appleton and Company.

Jackson, F. (1982). Epiphenomenal qualia. *Philosophical Quarterly* 32:127–136.

Kety, S.S. (1960). A biologist examines the mind and behaviour. *Science* 132:1861–1870.

Levine, J. (1983). Materialism and qualia: the explanatory gap. *Pacific Philosophical Quarterly*. 64:354–361.

Penfield, W. (1975). The mystery of the mind: a critical study of consciousness and the human brain. Princeton, New Jersey: Princeton University Press.

Russell, B. (1967). *The Problems of Philosophy*. Oxford: Oxford University Press.

——— (1984). *A History of Western Philosophy*. London: Counterpoint.

Ryle, G. (1949). *The Concept of Mind.* New York: Barnes and Noble.
Searle, J.R. (1994). *The Rediscovery of the Mind.* London: MIT Press.
Skinner, BF. (1965). *Science and Human Behaviour.* New York: The Free Press.
Wallace, E.R. (1988). Monistic dual aspect interactionism. *The Journal of Nervous and Mental Disease* 176:4–21.
Woolhouse, R.S., Francks, R., (Eds.) (1998). *G.W. Leibniz—Philosophical Texts.* Oxford: Oxford University Press.

Acknowledgement

I am grateful to the Melbourne philosopher Tamas Pataki for his helpful critique of this paper.

Mind over matter?
II: Implications for psychiatry

Published in *The Australian and New Zealand Journal of Psychiatry* 2001, 35:488–494

> 'It is a sign of weakness to combine empirical and logical arguments, for the latter, if valid, make the former superfluous.'
>
> Bertrand Russell (1984)

In the preceding paper Schimmel (2001) offered the following two propositions:

1. The faculty of mind is contingent upon the functioning human brain; in this sense mind and brain constitute two aspects of a unity. At a fundamental level there appears to be an 'identity' between specific mental states and specific brain states upon which they are contingent
2. Any attempt to explain the subjective essence of a mental state or process in terms of a brain state or process must inevitably fail as it leaves out the 'mind' that we seek to explain. Discourse about mental states is not reducible to discourse about brain states, and therefore brain states and mind states are not identical. (If *x* is identical to *y* then any property of *x* is also a property of *y*, and vice versa. Subjective mental events and objective brain events have distinct and differing properties.)

The preceding paper suggested that there are good grounds for accepting both of these propositions: 1) on the basis that it is the hypothesis that best fits the currently available scientific data and 2) on the basis that it is a self-evident truth. It also acknowledged the logical difficulty in entertaining both propositions simultaneously. Strictly speaking they do not constitute a solution to the 'mind-brain' problem, which as a metaphysical problem may be insoluble. They are proposed as the most satisfactory formulation of the problem possible given the limitations of our knowledge and/or understanding.

This second paper argues that, if these paradoxical propositions are accepted, they carry important theoretical and practical implications for concepts of causal explanation and etiology as they are applied to the mind and psychiatric disorders.

Causality and a unity theory

If we accept Proposition 1, that mental states and brain states constitute 'double aspects' of a unity, this suggests that in some fundamental way they are the same thing, or they arise as different manifestations of a unitary phenomenon (double aspect theory). If they constitute such a fundamental unity then one cannot simply be said to cause the other. We may say that the existence of mind is contingent upon the existence of certain states of the brain, but it seems doubtful that it can be meaningfully said that brain states cause the mind states that they 'co-exist' with, or for that matter, that mind states cause the brain states that they 'co-exist' with. Rather we might say mind states *are* the brain states that they 'co-exist' with.

Despite apparent widespread acceptance of some form of identity or unity theory within science in general and psychiatry in particular, its potential incompatibility with the idea that, at a given moment in time, mental activity is caused by brain activity (rather than simply contingent upon it) is apparently not often appreciated. Discourse and practice in psychiatry often carry an implicit assumption of brain activity causing mental activity; sometimes to the extent of relegating mind to the position of an epiphenomenon. Consider, for example, a clinician who tells a depressed patient (in whom there are no specific primary organic factors), that the depression is caused by a 'biochemical imbalance' in the brain. This statement recognizes the existence of something of the mind (the experience of depression), while relegating this to a secondary, or 'epiphenomenal', role to brain biochemistry. It suggests that the patient's mental experience of depression (the same argument holds for any mental experience), is caused by a set of other (whether observed or presumed) physical events taking place within the brain. However, it would make just as much, or just as little, sense to say that the experience of depression was causing the biochemistry or physiology of the brain to become disturbed. Within the framework of a unity, identity, or double aspect theory, neither of these propositions is logically defensible as it stands.

To the extent that a theory of mind is epiphenomenal it attributes causality to the brain, and excludes the attribution of causality to the mind, but if we are serious about some form of unity theory, it follows that in the unfolding sequence of brain/mind events, mental events have, in principle, the same causal status as brain events. As stated, mental events cannot simply be regarded as caused by the activity of the brain, because mental events *are* the activity of the brain.

If it is incoherent to speak of brain activity causing mental activity (at least in cross-sectional time), how then are we to speak about causality, and by implication etiology, in relation to brain and mind, and to psychiatric disorder? I suggest causality is most usefully considered in relation to the 'mind-brain system' as a whole, and if formulations of psychiatric causality are proposed, they must be consistent with concepts of causality employed in science generally. Within a dynamic system, evidence for causality is found in the identification of a set of reliable antecedent conditions/events that would seem to, or can be utilised to, predict subsequent conditions/events. The concept of causality carries the idea of something over and above this temporal juxtaposition of events, and a theory of cause is a formulation as to what this something is. Implicit in the concept of cause in a dynamic system is the passage of a period of time, however brief or infinitesimal.

To say that the brain events cannot be considered to cause mental events is not to say that identified events that cause change or disturbance in the brain do not cause change or disturbance in the mind; it is obvious that they do. Equally, identified events which cause change or disturbance in the mind cause a corresponding change or disturbance in the brain. The situation might be represented symbolically as follows, where M*e* stands for a 'mental event' and B*e* stands for the 'brain event' upon which that mental event is contingent:

Me1		Me2
	time→	
Be1		Be2

If a cause can be conceptualized as operating upon the mind to produce M*e*1 it *simultaneously* produces B*e*1. If a cause can be conceptualized as operating upon the brain to produce B*e*1 it *simultaneously* produces M*e*1. M*e*1/B*e*1 may then act causally to produce a second event in the 'mind-brain system', M*e*2/B*e*2. Of course, while all mental events will be contingent upon brain events, not all brain events need be linked with contingent mental events. For example, the following sequence is possible: B*e* (n) → B*e* (n+1)/M*e* (n+1).

To consider an example of the construction of a simple, but valid, causal model: a patient sustains a head injury with subsequent emotional disturbance and memory loss. There is a case for supposing that the immediate and determinate cause of the mental disorder is the physical injury. This conclusion is suggested by the fact that an unusual physical event, the head injury, was followed by, and seemed linked with, a disturbance of mental function. The cause is conceptualized as acting in longitudinal time. That the head injury was the cause of the disturbance would seem a reasonable working hypothesis, and for practical purposes might be regarded as confirmed on the basis of supporting evidence, for example: 1) evidence of physical damage to the brain resulting from the injury, and 2) the fact that similar mental disturbance has been observed in the past to be associated with the sort of injury to the brain sustained by the patient. That events of apparent cause and effect have previously conformed to a similar pattern supports the assumption of cause and effect on this occasion. Such a pattern may justify the formation of an inductive theory of causes and effects of this type.

If the brain injury was a random event outside the patient's control, then we have an example of an unintentional and physical brain-impinging event causing a disturbance in the 'mind-brain system'. In this instance a commonsense understanding of causality would not emphasise the mind, but rather emphasise that there was an identified *physical* cause. It would make common sense to say that the cause *operated via its impact upon the brain, leading to a disturbance of the mind-brain function.*

Consider, in a similar way, an event impacting upon the 'mind-brain system' that would usually be described as operating via the mind. A person, following news of a bereavement, is precipitated over a period of weeks into a melancholic depression. In this situation support for the hypothesis that the bereavement was the proximate and determinate causal factor might be gained from: 1) evidence from the patient's description of his/her experience of a link between the bereavement and the depression, and 2) the fact that similar mental disturbance has previously been observed associated with the experience of bereavement.

The identified causal factor, the bereavement, is a piece of knowledge or something given to awareness. Its impact derives from its *meaning* for the patient in terms of his mental life and social matrix of relationship. It is an essentially mind-impinging event causing a disturbance of the 'mind-brain system'. Although our mind-brain theory entails that there will be a neural 'substrate' of this meaningful impact, a commonsense understanding of causality would not emphasise the brain, but rather emphasise that there was an identified *mental* cause. It would make common sense to say that the cause *operated via its impact upon the mind, leading to a disturbance of the mind-brain function.*

There is both meaning and economy in saying that the effect of the head injury is via the brain, and the effect of the bereavement is via the mind. It would make little sense to say that the effect of the head injury was via the mind and the effect of the bereavement was via the brain.

The bereavement example is more complex than the head injury, because bereavements are a less reliable cause of depression than head injuries are of impaired mental function. So, in the bereavement example there must also be important vulnerability factor(s) within the patient. Assuming there are no specific organic factors contributing to vulnerability, then because the cause can be conceptualized as operating via the mind, it follows that the vulnerability factor(s) *must* also be able to be conceptualized as existing within the mind; logically it cannot be otherwise. This is simply to recognize that a bereavement can only impact upon a mind if it is experienced as meaningful. It is implicit in our mind-brain identity theory that the vulnerability factor(s) must also be represented in the brain, but if we wish to conceptualize the etiology of the depression in this particular situation we can only *meaningfully* do so in terms of the interaction of the news of the bereavement and the vulnerability within the patient's *mind*. The logical implication of this is that an etiological formulation based on identified neural processes, although possible in theory, will lack meaning (see below).

Etiology and a unity theory

If causality is to be considered in the genesis of psychiatric conditions then, as argued, this can only be done through the exploration of putative antecedent conditions or forces that lead to apparent alterations in the mind-brain system. Given that etiology represents the sum of causal factors the same argument applies to the consideration of etiology.

Related to the tendency within psychiatry to relegate mind to an epiphenomenal position rather than to accept the implications of a unitary theory, is the assumption that evidence of physical brain disturbance is sufficient to establish a physical etiology for a mental illness.

In principle a unitary theory predicts that any mental 'disturbance' is accompanied by a corresponding 'disturbance' of that part of the brain that underlies mentation, and vice-versa. It follows that, in principle, neither the presence of brain disturbance nor the presence of mental disturbance would, in itself, be sufficient to establish either a physical or mental etiology. Some other evidence will always be necessary.

The presence of physical brain disturbance alone can constitute reasonable and sufficient evidence of a physical etiology, only if that physical disturbance is in some way characteristic (pathognomonic) of a proven physical etiology. For example, the presence of the characteristic morphological changes of Alzheimer's disease in a patient with clinical dementia would seem a reasonable basis upon which to make this diagnosis, and to assume the operation of the physical etiological factors (known or unknown) associated with this disorder.

Obviously, the presence of apparently irreversible structural changes influencing brain function is *suggestive* of possible physical etiology, however factors operating via the mind cannot be dismissed without further evidence. If we consider schizophrenia, it is often assumed that because apparently pathological changes can reliably be detected in the brains of patients with this clinical diagnosis, then the etiology of the disorder must be 'physical' in the first instance, even if the specific nature of the purported physical cause(s) is not known. If the structural changes detected in the brain have an irreversible aspect, then in a commonsense way we might say that these changes are the immediate cause of the disturbed mind-brain function, but this does not establish etiology. Unless the changes can be recognized to be a consequence of a proven physical etiology, the possibility cannot be excluded that they represent the manifestations of the impingement of some 'psychosocial' factors, such as the developmental matrix of relationships. At present it would seem that the supporting evidence that would establish schizophrenia as a disorder of proven physical etiology in all, or even many, cases is lacking.

If the logical constraints upon establishing grounds for causal and etiological theories within the mind-brain system that have been put forward here are valid, they are not widely recognized within the psychiatric literature. Journals frequently publish papers where inference that etiology is 'biological' is made on the grounds that some biological, brain feature of a mental disorder has been (apparently) reliably identified. Mental illnesses are frequently reduced to 'neural' illnesses: consider the following opening sentence of a paper on brain imaging in psychiatry, and published in *Science* (Andreasen 1988). 'Psychiatrists have known for at least 100 years that mental illnesses must be fundamentally due to perturbations of normal neural activity in the brain.' While this statement may at first glance seem plausible this is appearance rather than reality. 'Fundamentally due to' suggests a cause, and as already argued there is logical difficulty in the description of brain events as causing mental events per se.

Even if we gloss over this 'in principle' logical difficulty, there is still no apparent reason why brain events are always more 'fundamental' than mental events. In this quotation the mental events in question are mental illnesses, and the brain events are 'perturbations of normal neural activity'. As has been argued, if some kind of irreversible neural disturbance were present, it might make sense to speak of a mental illness being 'fundamentally due to' this neural disturbance in cross-sectional time. However, this would not, in itself, establish that the mental illness was 'fundamentally due to' some physical/neural causal etiological factor. Furthermore, if no such irreversible change in brain structure or function is present in a particular mental illness, no prima facie case exists to support the claim that the neural events *must* be more fundamental than the mental events. There is greater explanatory economy to say, of at least some mental illnesses, that they are fundamentally due to perturbations of 'normal' psychological activity. *Whether a description using neural terms or mentalistic terms has the greatest utility in formulating a 'fundamental' explanation depends on the nature of the mental illness.*

The proper study of the mind

Turning now to Proposition 2, as stated at the beginning of the paper; if we accept that neuroscientific data and the data of mental experience are two different windows upon the unity referred to as the 'mind-brain system', we are left with the mystery that they appear to constitute ontologically distinct points of view. It follows that discourse in terms of one cannot be reduced to the other, and the two are not simply interchangeable, a reality which often seems to be lost sight of. It may be that the best we can hope to achieve is a descriptive correlation between the two. Neuroscience can, at least in theory, tell us a great deal about the neural correlates of a conscious experience, but it cannot tell us, at least not directly, anything about the inherent nature of that experience.

Despite those such as Kendell (1993) who reject the term 'mental illness' in favour of 'psychiatric illness' (Kendell rejects the concept of 'mental' in favour of the description 'psychiatric'), mental illnesses are called mental illnesses for a good commonsense reason; namely that they are, for the most part at least, experienced in the mind. The construct 'mental illness' reflects this fact, and from the patient's viewpoint the existence of such an 'illness' state is established through his/her awareness of parameters that reflect mental activity, either directly ('psychological symptoms') or indirectly ('behavioural signs').

Causal and etiological theories in psychiatry are constructed in terms of mental processes, brain processes, or both together (attempts to establish behavioural or sociological etiological theories are usually instances of theories framed in terms of subjective meaning, that is in terms of the mind). In practice the patient usually experiences, and the psychiatrist often judges, the presence of mental disturbance in terms of subjectively meaningful 'mental' phenomena. In these situations, only etiological formulations in terms of mental processes will be of the same ontological order as the primary phenomena under consideration.

In a patient where an etiological formulation in terms of mental process is possible, this will inevitably be more meaningful (*so long as the formulation is a correct one*), and therefore offer greater coherence in the particular case, than an etiological formulation in terms of brain process. A formulation in terms of the mind avoids falling into the ontological 'explanatory gap'. In other patients etiological formulation in terms of mental processes is either not possible or insufficient. Such cases require etiological theories formulated in part or whole in terms of primary brain processes. To the extent that it is not possible to formulate a *sufficient* explanation in mentalistic terms (that is in terms of meaning, or the 'dynamics' of the mind), then further explanation must be sought in terms of neurophysiological processes in the brain that have an independent aspect. A factor(s) extraneous to the inherently integrated mind-brain system, must be exerting an effect via the brain. That is, a physical/organic factor is added to the sequence M*e*1/B*e*1 – M*e*2/B*e*2, and is exerting its effect via 'B'. For example, in a state of alcohol intoxication, a factor operating independently of the normal integration of the mind-brain system introduces an element of randomness into the system. It might be predicted that this randomness would be detected as an interference with mental process, and experience confirms that mental capacities are diminished in alcohol intoxication. Similarly, the symbolic richness and meaningfulness of the world of a patient with Alzheimer's disease gradually diminishes with the progression of the disease.

In the hypothetical case of the patient who became depressed following news of a bereavement, it is in theory possible to describe the development of the depressive state of the 'mind-brain system' in neural terms. This would involve documenting the sequence of neurophysiological events, presumably involving many millions of neurons, over time. Such a task would hardly be practical, but an alternative would be to formulate a simplified model documenting the general patterns of brain activity. If such processes can be documented in the brain, then could the vulnerability to depression be conceptualized as residing in the brain? While it must in theory be possible to conceptualize the vulnerability of the 'mind-brain system' to depression in neural terms, as already suggested such conceptualization will lack meaning.

Neural processes that underlie the presentation of apparent mental disturbance or disorder, must presumably either be part of an ongoing sequence of integrated mind-brain activity, or represent a primary organic pathology. Old age, for example, is a specific organic factor that, being linked with a general impairment of cerebral function, may contribute to the vulnerability to depression. If we assume, in our patient, the absence of significant organic etiological factors requiring description primarily in neural terms, then as has been argued, because bereavement is an experience that impacts upon the mind, the patient's vulnerability to the experience must be able to be conceptualized in mentalistic terms (presumably in terms of the nature of the patient's attachments). *The premorbid state of cerebral functioning that confers vulnerability to depression is presumably, therefore, the neurophysiological correlate of the premorbid state of mental functioning that confers the vulnerability to depression.*

It is evident that, in this hypothetical case, only explanation in terms of psychological processes, including the psychological vulnerability factors within the patient's mind, will lead to an etiological formulation which is inherently meaningful (in the sense of offering understanding rather than a 'mechanistic' material explanation), and also potentially meaningful to the patient (whether in fact such a correct formulation is meaningful to a patient will depend upon his/her capacity to understand it). However accurate any model of the process of the patient's altered brain function over time might be, any attempt to employ it in a comprehensive explanatory sense will inevitably take on an arbitrary and reductive quality. It will not be inherently obvious how the documented brain phenomena 'explain' the mind phenomena (the patient's experience), because the relationship between them is one of correlation established by observation, rather than one established on the basis of the apprehension of inherently meaningful links.

To restate, because of the ontological 'explanatory gap' between formulations in mentalistic terms and formulations in neural terms, a formulation in terms of mind will, *if correct*, introduce or elucidate the meaning of the patient's experience and behaviour in a way that 'explanation' in terms of constitution or neurophysiology cannot do. I emphasize 'if correct' because: 1) an etiological formulation in terms of mental processes may be more or less correct or incorrect. An incorrect formulation will not, of course, elucidate the meaning of the patient's experience and behaviour, and may obscure that meaning. 2) I am not suggesting that etiological formulation in terms of mental process is possible for all mental illness, but in any instance where such formulation is possible it will inevitably offer a level of understanding which formulation in terms of neural processes cannot.

Perhaps our hypothetical depressed patient consults the clinician who formulates the cause of his depression as a 'a biochemical imbalance in the brain'. It may not be unreasonable to postulate that there is a state of biochemical 'imbalance' in the patient's brain, but can this in any sense logically constitute the 'cause' of the disorder?

The fact that what initiated the 'disorder' (bereavement) is meaningfully conceptualized in mentalistic terms (the dynamics of the mind), would suggest seeking understanding of the developing state, at least in the first instance, in terms of processes that can be characterized in mentalistic terms. This would mean adopting a working hypothesis that the 'biochemical imbalance' is the brain representation in cross-sectional time of a disturbance within an *integrated* mind-brain system. So long as a *sufficient* explanation of the patient's clinical presentation can be formulated in mentalistic terms, then from a logical viewpoint an etiological formulation in terms of neurophysiology, however accurate, remains redundant to meaningful explanation. It may be a valid explanation but it will not be a meaningful one. One might say therefore that it would lack explanatory power.

A principle of *explanatory economy* could be postulated as follows: it is only when formulation in terms of the dynamics of the mind falls short of providing adequate explanation that it becomes necessary to postulate a neurophysiological causal factor acting independently of an integrated mind-brain system. It would contradict this principle to postulate an explanation primarily in neurophysiological terms in the absence of evidence that some primary and therefore independent pathophysiological process has supervened.

The presence of biochemical disturbance alone in the brains of depressed patients is not sufficient to justify the assumption of a physical/neural etiology. Supporting evidence will always be required. Where a 'biochemical imbalance' idea is employed as a kind of a priori etiological 'theory', such reasoning is inimical to the process of inquiry and analysis, in other words the process of thinking about, that is necessary to elucidate meaning. In practice the acceptance of this kind of 'biochemical' thinking about, for example, depression is often associated with a closure that fails to recognize the possibility of other, potentially more coherent, and clinically more fruitful, avenues of investigation.

The invocation of *any* etiological theory without specific and sufficient supporting evidence contributes to premature closure. The 'concrete' and measurable aspect of brain events in comparison to mental events, may make neural formulations appear attractive, perhaps because they seem easier to grasp, than psychological formulations, but as our theory of mind and brain assumes that neural disturbance and mental disturbance accompany one another, we should be aware of the fallacy of invoking physical/organic etiological theories on the basis of identified neural disturbance without supporting evidence.

I have referred to the possibility of formulating disturbances in the 'mind-brain system' either in terms of neurophysiological processes or in terms of mental processes, the 'dynamics of the mind'. The nature of the empirical methods employed in order to characterize neurophysiological processes are well known and their conceptual validity apprehended relatively easily. In contrast the empirical methods employed in order to characterize dynamic mental processes are less well known, and their conceptual validity apprehended with greater difficulty. They are essentially the elements of an analytic approach to mental phenomena which seeks to establish meaning, whether employed in psychoanalysis, in analytic psychotherapy, or in an observational context. This paper has assumed the validity of such 'psycho-analytic' methods, but there remains contention within psychiatry as to the validly of knowledge attained by interpretive methods. *Yet it is self-evident that meaning is only conferred upon human experience through interpretation.* Pataki (p. 5) points to the 'explanatory work' done in ordinary narrative 'by commonsense "mentalistic" concepts like love, hatred, fear, belief, feelings of weakness and dependence, and so on. These are the concepts we commonly use to make sense of ourselves and others. They are immensely rich concepts', and they are 'basic, in (roughly) this sense: it is impossible to see how any description of human action (or of society) can be made without them and their kind in a way which will preserve its subject.'

It is beyond the scope of the paper to enter further into the question of how the validity of knowledge attained through interpretive methods may be established. This would lead inevitably to consideration of the validity of the concept of 'unconscious' mental processes.

Mind over matter?

I believe that there is a bias within psychiatry against the investigation of the patient's mind. Without any conceptualization of the dynamic processes occurring within the disordered mind, it is difficult to formulate any etiological theory that takes factors operating via the mind into account, and difficult to approach treatment via the mind. This results in an explanatory vacuum which neural models are often invoked to fill. Wherever it is possible to formulate a correct etiology in terms of mental processes, and if a clinician is able to do so, then, for the reasons outlined, this will possess a maximum explanatory economy. It will certainly be meaningful in a way that a 'neural' formulation cannot be.

This does not amount to suggesting that mind is more important in psychiatry than brain. A psychiatrist needs to understand about brains and about minds, and there are different forms of psychiatric practice. It is an argument for the utility of giving consideration to the processes taking place within the patient's mind. I have attempted to base this argument upon 1) what seems a reasonable formulation of the mind-brain problem given current knowledge, and 2) drawing out the implications of this formulation in clinical situations. The main conclusions reached are: a) that neural brain activity cannot in principle be regarded as causing mental activity (or vice-versa), and therefore more evidence or information will need to be considered if the causal relationships between 'mind' factors and 'brain' factors are to be elucidated in a particular case, or in a particular psychiatric condition, and b) that because of the 'explanatory gap' between descriptions in mentalistic terms and descriptions in neurophysiological terms, wherever an explanatory formulation of a mental illness in mentalistic terms is possible, this will carry greater explanatory power (meaning) than a formulation in terms of disturbed neural function. If an explanatory formulation in terms of mental processes does not seem possible, or is insufficient, then a formulation in terms of some other primary neural process is necessary.

We have two windows to view the 'mind-brain system', observation of the brain and observation of the mind. The observation of mental contents and processes, either through introspection or second person observation, offers a privileged and readily available point of access. It is both the obvious and the logical point to begin investigation into the nature of mental disturbance. Despite this psychiatry appears increasingly preoccupied with the idea of getting at some 'essence' of mental disorder through brain research. While we must have an understanding of the manifestations of primary disturbances of the brain in order to understand many psychiatric illnesses, and while we must have an understanding of the pathophysiology of the brain that supervenes in some psychiatric illnesses, this does not mean that a brain focus will serve well to gain understanding of all psychiatric illnesses. Because of the 'explanatory gap' we are faced with when we try and understand mind in terms of brain, a 'mind' focus will better serve understanding in the absence of specific independent or irreversible pathophysiological disturbances.

References

Russell, B. (1984). *A History of Western Philosophy* (pp. 623–633). London: Counterpoint.

Schimmel, P. (2001). Mind over matter? I: philosophical aspects of the mind-brain problem. *Australian and New Zealand Journal of Psychiatry* 35:481–487.

Andreasen, N.C. (1988). Brain imaging: applications in psychiatry. *Science* 239:1381–1388.

Kendell, R.E. (1993). The nature of psychiatric disorders. In R.E. Kendell & A.K. Zealley (Eds.). *Companion to Psychiatric Studies* (Edition 5). Edinburgh: Churchill Livingston.

Pataki, T. (1996). Psychoanalysis, psychiatry, philosophy. *Quadrant* 40(4):52–63.

Acknowledgement

I am grateful to the Melbourne philosopher Tamas Pataki for his helpful critique of this paper.

A tribute to Neville Symington

I was not in analysis or supervision with Neville, but his thinking had a great influence on me, which I would like to acknowledge.

Effective psychoanalysis leads to a freedom to speak one's thoughts, and Neville had the capacity to say what he thought without fear or favour, not always to the appreciation of others.

We enter analysis with some sense of an inner sickness, and it seems Neville was fortunate in his choice of John Klauber as his analyst. Of course, a good psychoanalysis doesn't cure everything, but it's the best start we have. In Neville's *A Different Path* (2016) I found this about his analysis: Enid Balint thought the best analyst for Neville would be John Klauber:

> 'After I had been speaking to him for some time he said: Do you mind if I be entirely frank with you … ?'
> 'No please do I said in terror.'
> 'I think you are very ill, you know'
> 'I almost cried with relief.' (2016 p. 271)

In Neville's book I was also impressed to read that in response to the situation in his mind, he had decided to read D.H. Lawrence: *The White Peacock*, *Sons and Lovers*, *Lady Chatterley's Lover*, and *Women in Love*. (ibid. p. 202). These are powerful novels which can have such an impact on a developing or stuck mind.

As I've said, Neville's thinking had a great influence, for example, in his insistence that psychoanalysis was not a matter of 4 or 5 sessions/week.

Neville's analysis of what is of the essence in psychoanalytic work, and what is peripheral, such as frequency of sessions and the couch, was most helpful.

I came to a personal realization, that the only place a therapist can ensure an analytic process is within his or her own mind. The rest is up to the communication capacity of the therapist, to the patient, and to the gods.

Another iconoclastic view: Neville pointing out that we speak of training, but one trains rats!

Neville and his wife Joan were much influenced by the thinking of Wilfred Bion, about whom he sometimes recounted amusing anecdotes. I see similarities between the two men, not least that both had been shipped off to boarding school at a tender age.

Neville, when on form, was a most compelling speaker. I mined his talks for everything I could get.

Most important however were his books. For me the best were *The Analytic Experience: Lectures from the Tavistock*, and *Narcissism: A New Theory*. I recognize the genius in these works, but for some reason they are not drawn upon in our 'training' of candidates.

Neville was a man of achievement. Behind this man of achievement was a woman of achievement, his wife Joan.

Together they collaborated on writing another work of genius; a book on Wilfred Bion.

There is sadness at Neville's passing, mitigated by the fact that his legacy is there for all of us. I mourn the loss of an outstanding thinker, with an independent mind. I note his courage towards the end.

Reference

Symington, N. (2016). *A Different Path: An Emotional Autobiography*. London: Karnac.

A TRIBUTE TO NEVILLE SYMINGTON

www.ingramcontent.com/pod-product-compliance
Lightning Source LLC
Chambersburg PA
CBHW062125020426
42335CB00013B/1105

9781956864205